ANNA JAMES

Reykjavik, Iceland Travel Guide

First published by Oak Publisher 2024

Copyright © 2024 by Anna James

All rights reserved. No part of this publication may be reproduced, stored or transmitted in any form or by any means, electronic, mechanical, photocopying, recording, scanning, or otherwise without written permission from the publisher. It is illegal to copy this book, post it to a website, or distribute it by any other means without permission.

First edition

This book was professionally typeset on Reedsy. Find out more at reedsy.com

Contents

Introduction	1
Getting to Reykjavik	12
Exploring Reykjavik	40
Outdoor Activities in Reykjavik	81
Day Trips from Reykjavik	144
Local Cuisine and Dining	184
Accommodations	211
Practical Information	233
Conclusion	249

Introduction

Welcome to Reykjavik

Reykjavik, the capital and largest city of Iceland, is a vibrant and unique destination that perfectly blends modern urban culture with breathtaking natural landscapes. As the northernmost capital of the world, Reykjavik offers visitors an array of experiences, from its rich history and thriving arts scene to its stunning outdoor adventures.

A City of Contrasts

Reykjavik is known for its colorful architecture, cozy cafes, and welcoming atmosphere. The city is not just the political and cultural heart of Iceland; it's also a gateway to incredible natural wonders. Whether you're wandering the charming streets, soaking in geothermal hot springs, or exploring the rugged landscapes of the surrounding countryside, Reykjavik promises an unforgettable experience.

Embrace the Local Culture

The city is deeply rooted in Norse history and culture, and you'll find this reflected in its museums, art galleries, and cultural events. Reykjavik's vibrant nightlife and culinary scene showcase local traditions and modern influences, offering everything from traditional Icelandic dishes to innovative cuisine crafted from fresh, local ingredients.

Adventure Awaits

For outdoor enthusiasts, Reykjavik serves as the perfect base to explore Iceland's stunning natural beauty. From the geothermal wonders of the Golden Circle to the dramatic landscapes of the South Coast, the options for adventure are limitless. Activities like whale watching, glacier hiking, and soaking in hot springs allow you to connect with Iceland's breathtaking nature.

The Perfect Year-Round Destination

Reykjavik is a year-round destination, with each season offering its unique charm. In winter, you can chase the enchanting Northern Lights, while summer brings nearly 24 hours of daylight, ideal for hiking and exploring. Regardless of when you visit, you'll find that Reykjavik's charm and the warmth of its people create an inviting atmosphere that keeps visitors coming back.

INTRODUCTION

Your Journey Starts Here

As you embark on your journey to Reykjavik, prepare to be captivated by its stunning landscapes, rich culture, and the warm hospitality of its residents. This travel guide will help you navigate the city's must-visit attractions and outdoor activities, ensuring you make the most of your time in this extraordinary destination. Welcome to Reykjavik—your adventure begins now!

Overview of Reykjavik

Reykjavik is not only the capital of Iceland but also the largest city in the country, serving as its cultural, economic, and political center. With a population of approximately 130,000, it is home to about one-third of Iceland's total population. This vibrant city combines a rich history with a modern urban lifestyle, making it an intriguing destination for visitors.

Geography and Climate

Nestled on the southwestern coast of Iceland, Reykjavik is surrounded by stunning natural beauty, including mountains, lava fields, and the Atlantic Ocean. The city's geographical location near the Mid-Atlantic Ridge contributes to its unique landscape, featuring geothermal hot springs and volcanic activity.

Reykjavik experiences a subarctic climate, characterized by mild winters and cool summers. The average temperature in winter hovers around -1°C (30°F), while summer temperatures can reach up to 15°C (59°F). The city enjoys long daylight hours during summer months, with nearly 24 hours of sunlight around the summer solstice, while winter brings the magic of the Northern Lights.

History and Culture

Reykjavik's history dates back to the settlement of Iceland in the 9th century when the first Norse settlers arrived. The city was officially founded in 1786 and has since evolved into a vibrant cultural hub. The name "Reykjavik," which means "Smoky Bay," refers to the steam rising from the geothermal hot springs in the area.

Culturally, Reykjavik is renowned for its artistic scene, with numerous galleries, theaters, and music venues. The city hosts various festivals throughout the year, including the Reykjavik Arts Festival and the Reykjavik International Film Festival, showcasing local and international talent.

Attractions

Reykjavik is home to several must-see attractions that highlight its unique character:

- Hallgrímskirkja: This iconic church is one of Reykjavik's most recognizable landmarks, offering panoramic views of the city from its tower.
   - Harpa Concert Hall: A stunning example of modern architecture, Harpa hosts concerts, events, and exhibitions, making it a cultural

centerpiece.

- National Museum of Iceland: This museum provides an in-depth look at Iceland's history and culture, featuring artifacts from the Viking era to modern times.

- Sun Voyager: A striking sculpture located by the waterfront, symbolizing exploration and discovery.

Outdoor Activities

Reykjavik is a gateway to numerous outdoor adventures. The city's location makes it easy to access breathtaking landscapes and unique natural phenomena. Popular outdoor activities include:

- Whale Watching: Tours depart from the Old Harbor, offering opportunities to see various whale species in their natural habitat.

- Geothermal Pools: Reykjavik boasts numerous public swimming pools and hot springs, including the famous Blue Lagoon, where visitors can relax and rejuvenate.

- Hiking and Nature Walks: Scenic trails are available nearby, including Mount Esja and the nature reserve of Heiðmörk, providing stunning views of the surrounding landscapes.

Culinary Scene

Reykjavik's culinary scene is diverse, with a focus on fresh, local ingredients. Visitors can enjoy traditional Icelandic dishes, such as lamb soup and seafood, alongside modern cuisine in trendy restaurants and cafes. The city is also known for its lively food markets, where you can sample local delicacies.

Best Time to Visit Reykjavik

Reykjavik, with its unique climate and varied seasonal offerings, can be a fantastic destination at any time of year. The best time to visit depends on your preferences for weather, activities, and local events. Here's a breakdown of what each season offers:

1. Winter (December to February)

- Weather: Temperatures range from -1°C to 4°C (30°F to 39°F). While it can be chilly, the presence of geothermal heat in the city makes it manageable.
　- Activities:
　- Northern Lights: Winter is the best time to witness the aurora borealis. Clear nights with minimal light pollution increase your chances of seeing this spectacular natural phenomenon.
　- Winter Sports: Nearby areas offer skiing, snowboarding, and snowmobiling opportunities.
　- Geothermal Pools: Enjoy relaxing in hot springs and geothermal pools, which are particularly inviting during the cold months.
　- Events: The Reykjavik Winter Lights Festival in February showcases art, culture, and lighting displays.

2. Spring (March to May)

- Weather: Temperatures gradually rise, ranging from 0°C to 10°C (32°F to 50°F). The days become longer, providing more sunlight.
　- Activities:
　- Bird Watching: Spring is an excellent time for birdwatching, especially for spotting puffins along the coast.

INTRODUCTION

 - Hiking: Trails start to open up as snow melts, making way for beautiful hikes in nearby nature reserves.
 - Whale Watching: Tours start up again in April, offering sightings of various whale species.
 - Events: The Reykjavik Art Festival and the Reykjavik Maritime Festival celebrate the city's culture and heritage.

3. Summer (June to August)

- Weather: Summer temperatures average between 10°C and 15°C (50°F to 59°F), with longer days and the phenomenon of midnight sun, where the sun hardly sets.
 - Activities:
 - Outdoor Adventures: Ideal for hiking, biking, and exploring the stunning landscapes surrounding the city, such as the Golden Circle and Snæfellsnes Peninsula.
 - Festivals: Enjoy various music and arts festivals, such as the Reykjavik Jazz Festival and the Reykjavik Pride celebration.
 - Fishing and Kayaking: Summer is perfect for fishing trips and kayaking in the surrounding waters.
 - Note: Summer is the peak tourist season, so expect larger crowds and higher accommodation prices.

4. Autumn (September to November)

- Weather: Temperatures begin to drop, ranging from 1°C to 10°C (34°F to 50°F). The changing leaves provide stunning scenery.
 - Activities:
 - Northern Lights: Similar to winter, autumn offers excellent opportunities for viewing the aurora borealis, especially in September and October.

- Harvest Season: Enjoy local cuisine featuring seasonal ingredients, such as fresh seafood and lamb.
  - Hiking and Nature Walks: Trails remain accessible, and the fall colors create beautiful landscapes for outdoor exploration.
  - Events: The Reykjavik Culture Night in August and the Reykjavik International Film Festival in late September highlight the city's vibrant arts scene.

Travel Tips for Visiting Reykjavik, Iceland

When planning your trip to Reykjavik, it's helpful to keep in mind some practical tips and insights that will enhance your experience. Here are essential travel tips for navigating the city and enjoying all it has to offer:

1. Dress Appropriately

- Layering is Key: The weather in Reykjavik can be unpredictable, so dress in layers. A waterproof jacket, thermal base layers, and sturdy footwear are essential, especially if you plan to explore the outdoors.
  - Swimwear: Don't forget your swimsuit if you plan to visit geothermal pools or hot springs!

INTRODUCTION

2. Embrace the Local Currency

- Currency: Iceland uses the Icelandic króna (ISK). While credit cards are widely accepted, having some cash on hand for small purchases or tips can be useful.
   - ATMs: ATMs are readily available throughout the city, and withdrawing cash is straightforward.

3. Transportation Tips

- Public Transport: Reykjavik has a reliable bus system (Strætó) that connects the city and surrounding areas. Purchase a bus card for convenience.
   - Walking and Biking: Many of the city's attractions are within walking distance of each other. Consider renting a bike to explore at your own pace.
   - Car Rentals: If you plan to venture outside the city, renting a car gives you the flexibility to explore Iceland's stunning landscapes.

4. Plan Your Outdoor Activities

- Book in Advance: Popular activities like whale watching, glacier tours, and northern lights excursions can fill up quickly, especially in peak season. Book your tours in advance.
   - Stay Flexible: Weather can change rapidly in Iceland. Be prepared to adjust your plans based on conditions, especially for outdoor activities.

5. Respect Nature and the Environment

- Follow Guidelines: Iceland's natural wonders are fragile. Stay on marked paths, and respect local guidelines to preserve the environment.
  - Leave No Trace: Always clean up after yourself and dispose of waste properly.

6. Experience Local Culture

- Try Traditional Cuisine: Sample Icelandic dishes like lamb soup, seafood, and skyr (a yogurt-like dairy product). Don't miss trying local street food at the famous hot dog stand, Bæjarins Beztu Pylsur.
  - Explore Museums and Galleries: Take time to visit Reykjavik's museums, such as the National Museum of Iceland and the Reykjavik Art Museum, to learn about the country's history and culture.

7. Stay Connected

- Wi-Fi Availability: Reykjavik has good internet connectivity, with free Wi-Fi available in many cafes, restaurants, and public spaces.
  - SIM Cards: If you need mobile data, consider purchasing a local SIM card from one of the many telecom providers in the city.

8. Safety and Health

- Emergency Numbers: The emergency number in Iceland is 112. Keep this in mind in case of any emergencies.
  - Health Insurance: Ensure you have adequate travel insurance that

covers health and emergencies during your trip.

9. Timing Your Visits

- Tourist Attractions: Popular sites can get crowded during peak hours. Try to visit major attractions early in the morning or later in the afternoon for a more enjoyable experience.
    - Daylight Hours: Be aware of daylight hours, especially during winter, when the days are much shorter. Plan your outdoor activities accordingly.

10. Enjoy the Midnight Sun or Northern Lights

- Midnight Sun: If you visit in summer, take advantage of the extended daylight hours for sightseeing and outdoor activities.
    - Northern Lights: If traveling in winter, keep an eye on the aurora forecast and be flexible with your plans to maximize your chances of witnessing the spectacular Northern Lights.

Getting to Reykjavik

Arriving in Iceland: A Guide for First-Time Travelers

Arriving in Iceland is an exciting experience, as the unique landscapes and vibrant culture await you. Here's a comprehensive guide to help you navigate your arrival in Reykjavik, including transportation options, airport information, and tips for getting settled.

1. Keflavik International Airport (KEF)

- Location: Keflavik International Airport is located about 50 kilometers (31 miles) southwest of Reykjavik.
  - Facilities: The airport is modern and equipped with essential amenities, including shops, restaurants, currency exchange, and car rental services. Free Wi-Fi is available throughout the terminal.

2. Transportation Options from the Airport to Reykjavik

- Airport Shuttle Services:
  - Flybus: A popular choice, the Flybus operates frequent shuttle services between the airport and Reykjavik. The buses are timed to coincide with flight arrivals, and the journey takes about 45 minutes.
  - Airport Direct: Another reliable shuttle service offering similar routes to Reykjavik. You can book tickets in advance online or at the airport.

- Private Transfers:
  - If you prefer a more personalized experience, you can book a private transfer or taxi. Taxis are available outside the arrivals area, but they can be more expensive than shuttle services.

- Rental Cars:
  - If you plan to explore Iceland outside Reykjavik, consider renting a car at the airport. Major car rental companies operate at Keflavik, and booking in advance is recommended, especially during peak season.

3. Customs and Immigration

- Passport Control: Upon arrival, you will need to present your passport for immigration checks. Ensure that your passport is valid for at least six months beyond your planned departure date from Iceland.

- Customs Regulations: Familiarize yourself with Iceland's customs regulations regarding prohibited items and duty-free allowances. Alcohol and tobacco can be purchased duty-free upon arrival.

4. Getting Settled in Reykjavik

- Accommodation:
    - Prior to your arrival, it's a good idea to book accommodation in Reykjavik. Options range from hotels and guesthouses to hostels and vacation rentals, catering to various budgets.

- Currency Exchange
    - The local currency is the Icelandic króna (ISK). Currency exchange services are available at the airport, but you can also withdraw cash from ATMs located in the city.

- Local SIM Cards:
    - If you need mobile data, consider purchasing a local SIM card at the airport or in Reykjavik. Major providers include Síminn, Vodafone, and Nova.

5. Orientation and First Impressions

- Exploring Reykjavik:
    - Once settled, take some time to explore the capital. Start with iconic landmarks such as Hallgrímskirkja, Harpa Concert Hall, and the Sun Voyager.

- Local Food:

- Experience Icelandic cuisine at local restaurants or cafes. Don't miss trying traditional dishes like lamb soup, seafood, and Icelandic hot dogs.

- Weather Awareness:
   - Be prepared for rapidly changing weather conditions. Carry a waterproof jacket and dress in layers to stay comfortable during your explorations.

6. Getting Around Reykjavik

- Public Transport:
   - Reykjavik has an efficient public bus system (Strætó) that connects the city with nearby areas. Purchase a bus card for convenience, or pay with a contactless credit card.

- Walking and Biking:
   - The city is pedestrian-friendly, and many attractions are within walking distance. Biking is also a popular way to explore Reykjavik.

7. Planning Your Itinerary

- Must-See Attractions:
   - Prioritize visits to landmarks like the National Museum of Iceland, Laugavegur shopping street, and the famous geothermal pools, such as the Blue Lagoon and local swimming pools.

- Day Trips:
  - Reykjavik is an excellent base for day trips to natural wonders like the Golden Circle, Snæfellsnes Peninsula, and the South Coast.

Keflavik International Airport (KEF): Your Gateway to Iceland

Keflavik International Airport (KEF) is Iceland's main international airport and serves as the primary gateway for travelers visiting the country. Here's a comprehensive overview of what you need to know about arriving at and navigating through KEF:

1. Airport Overview

- Location:
  - Keflavik International Airport is situated approximately 50 kilometers (31 miles) southwest of Reykjavik, the capital of Iceland.

- Terminal Information:
  - The airport has a single terminal that handles both international and domestic flights. It is well-organized, making it easy for travelers to navigate.

2. Getting to and from the Airport

- Transportation Options:
   - Airport Shuttle Services:
   - Flybus: Offers regular shuttle services between KEF and various locations in Reykjavik. The journey takes about 45 minutes. Tickets can be booked online or purchased at the airport.
   - Airport Direct: Another reliable shuttle service with frequent departures.
   - Private Transfers:
   - Pre-booked private transfers or taxis are available outside the arrivals area. While convenient, they can be more expensive than shuttle services.
   - Rental Cars:
   - Major car rental companies operate at KEF. It's advisable to book a rental car in advance, especially during peak tourist season.

3. Airport Facilities and Services

- Amenities:
   - Dining and Shopping: The airport features a variety of restaurants, cafes, and shops, including duty-free stores for alcohol, souvenirs, and Icelandic products.
   - Wi-Fi: Free Wi-Fi is available throughout the terminal, allowing you to stay connected during your time at the airport.
   - Luggage Services: Luggage storage and lost & found services are provided.

- Currency Exchange:
  - Currency exchange services are available at the airport, along with ATMs for cash withdrawals.

4. Customs and Immigration

- Passport Control:
  - Upon arrival, you will go through immigration control, where you will need to present your passport. Make sure it is valid for at least six months beyond your planned departure date.

- Customs Regulations:
  - Familiarize yourself with Iceland's customs regulations, including restrictions on certain items and duty-free allowances. Alcohol and tobacco can be purchased duty-free upon arrival.

5. Travel Tips for Arrival

- Plan Your Arrival Time:
  - Allow ample time for customs and immigration checks, especially during peak travel seasons.

- Transportation Arrangements:
  - If you have not pre-booked a shuttle or rental car, it's advisable to do so before your arrival to ensure a smooth transition to Reykjavik.

- Stay Informed:

- Keep an eye on flight information monitors for updates on arrivals and departures.

6. Accessibility

- Facilities for Passengers with Disabilities:
  - Keflavik International Airport is equipped with facilities for passengers with disabilities, including accessible restrooms, elevators, and assistance services.

Domestic Transport Options in Reykjavik and Iceland

Getting around Reykjavik and exploring other parts of Iceland is convenient, thanks to various domestic transport options. Here's an overview of the available transportation methods:

1. Public Transport in Reykjavik

- Buses (Strætó):
  - Reykjavik has an extensive bus network operated by Strætó. The buses are reliable and cover the city and surrounding areas.
  - Tickets: You can purchase single tickets, as well as a multi-ride card or a day pass. Tickets can be bought at bus terminals or via the Strætó app. The buses accept cashless payments via credit/debit cards.

- Frequency: Buses run regularly, but schedules may vary on weekends and holidays.

- Walking and Biking:
  - Reykjavik is a pedestrian-friendly city, and many attractions are within walking distance.
  - Biking: Several bike rental shops offer bicycles for rent, and dedicated bike lanes make cycling a safe option.

2. Taxi Services

- Taxis:
  - Taxis are widely available throughout Reykjavik. They can be hailed on the street or booked via phone or taxi apps.
  - Fare Structure: Taxis operate on a meter system, and prices can vary based on distance and time of day. Note that taxi fares can be higher than public transport.

3. Car Rentals

- Rental Companies:
  - Major car rental companies operate in Reykjavik and at Keflavik International Airport. Renting a car is a popular option for travelers looking to explore Iceland's stunning landscapes.
  - Booking: It's recommended to book your car in advance, especially during peak tourist season.

- Driving in Iceland:
  - Iceland has well-maintained roads, but some remote areas may require a 4x4 vehicle due to gravel roads and challenging terrain. Always check road conditions, especially in winter.

4. Domestic Flights

- Air Iceland Connect:
  - Domestic flights are available from Reykjavik to various locations across Iceland, including Akureyri, Egilsstaðir, and Ísafjörður.
  - Duration: Flights are usually short (ranging from 45 minutes to 1.5 hours), making this an efficient option for reaching distant areas.

5. Tours and Excursions

- Day Tours:
  - Many companies offer guided tours from Reykjavik to popular destinations such as the Golden Circle, South Coast, and Snæfellsnes Peninsula.
  - These tours often include transportation, making them a convenient way to explore without the need for a rental car.

6. Long-Distance Buses

- Bus Services:
  - For traveling between cities or to popular tourist destinations, long-distance bus services like Sterna and Reykjavik Excursions are available.
  - Tickets: Tickets can be purchased online or at bus terminals. These buses often connect Reykjavik to other regions and major tourist attractions.

7. Ferries

- Ferry Services:
  - Ferries operate from Reykjavik to several nearby islands, including Viðey and the Westman Islands.
  - Reservations: It's advisable to book your ferry tickets in advance, especially during peak travel times.

Getting Around Reykjavik: A Comprehensive Guide

Reykjavik, Iceland's capital, is a compact and walkable city, making it relatively easy to explore. Here's a detailed guide to the various options for getting around Reykjavik, whether you prefer public transport, biking, or driving.

1. Walking

- Pedestrian-Friendly:
  - Reykjavik's city center is highly pedestrian-friendly, with many attractions, shops, and restaurants within walking distance. Walking is one of the best ways to experience the city's charm.

- Key Attractions:
  - Popular sights like Hallgrímskirkja, Harpa Concert Hall, the Sun Voyager, and Laugavegur shopping street are all easily accessible on foot.

2. Biking

- Bike Rentals:
  - Several rental shops throughout Reykjavik offer bicycles for rent. This is a great way to explore the city at your own pace.

- Bike Lanes:
  - Reykjavik has dedicated bike lanes, making cycling a safe and enjoyable option. The city also features scenic routes along the coastline and through parks.

3. Public Transport (Buses)

- Strætó Buses:
  - Reykjavik has an efficient public bus system operated by Strætó, which connects the city and nearby suburbs.

- Routes and Frequency:
  - Buses cover key areas, including the city center, neighborhoods, and popular attractions. While service is frequent, it may vary on weekends and holidays.

- Ticketing:
  - You can purchase single tickets, multi-ride cards, or day passes. Tickets are available at bus terminals and via the Strætó app. The buses accept cashless payments with credit or debit cards.

4. Taxis

- Availability:
  - Taxis are widely available in Reykjavik and can be hailed on the street, booked via phone, or through taxi apps.

- Fare Structure:
  - Taxis operate on a meter system, and fares can vary based on distance and time of day. Keep in mind that taxi fares can be higher than public transport.

5. Car Rentals

- Rental Companies:
    - Major car rental companies have locations in Reykjavik and at Keflavik International Airport. Renting a car is convenient if you plan to explore areas outside the city.

- Driving Conditions:
    - Reykjavik has well-maintained roads, but always check road conditions if you plan to drive to more remote locations.

6. Airport Transfers

- Airport Shuttle Services:
    - Services like Flybus and Airport Direct operate shuttles between Keflavik International Airport and various locations in Reykjavik. These shuttles are a convenient option for getting to and from the airport.

- Private Transfers:
    - Pre-booked private transfers are also available for a more personalized experience.

7. Guided Tours

- Tour Operators:
    - Many companies offer guided tours of Reykjavik and surrounding areas. These tours often include transportation, making it easy to visit multiple attractions without worrying about logistics.

8. Accessibility

- Facilities for Passengers with Disabilities:
  - Reykjavik is working to improve accessibility, with many buses and public spaces designed to accommodate passengers with disabilities. Check with your transport provider for specific accessibility options.

Public Transportation in Reykjavik: A Detailed Guide

Reykjavik's public transportation system is efficient, reliable, and user-friendly, making it easy for visitors to explore the city and its surrounding areas. Here's a comprehensive overview of the public transport options available in Reykjavik:

1. Strætó Buses

- Overview:
  - Strætó is Reykjavik's public bus service, operating an extensive network of routes throughout the city and surrounding suburbs. The buses are a convenient way to reach key attractions, neighborhoods, and the greater capital area.

- Routes:
  - The bus network includes numerous lines connecting various parts of the city, including popular destinations such as:

- Harpa Concert Hall
  - Hallgrímskirkja
  - Laugavegur shopping street
  - Reykjavik's city center
  - Nearby suburbs like Kópavogur and Garðabær

- Frequency:
  - Buses run frequently during the day, though schedules may vary on weekends and holidays. Most routes operate from early morning until late at night, but it's advisable to check the timetable for specific lines.

2. Ticketing and Fare System

- Types of Tickets:
  - Single Ticket: Valid for one journey and must be used within 75 minutes from the time of validation.
  - Multi-Ride Card: Offers multiple rides at a discounted rate, perfect for frequent travelers.
  - Day Pass: Unlimited travel on the bus network for a single day.

- Purchasing Tickets:
  - Tickets can be purchased at bus terminals or directly on the bus (cashless payments via credit/debit cards only). The Strætó app also allows for easy ticket purchasing and route planning.

- Validation:
  - Ensure to validate your ticket upon boarding. Keep your ticket handy, as bus staff may check for valid tickets during your journey.

3. Bus Stops and Information

- Bus Stops:
    - Bus stops are clearly marked throughout the city, with information about routes, schedules, and real-time arrival updates.

- Route Planning:
    - The Strætó app and website provide route maps, timetables, and trip planners to help you navigate the bus system efficiently. Additionally, many bus stops have screens displaying real-time arrival information.

4. Accessibility

- Facilities for Passengers with Disabilities:
    - Most buses are equipped with features to assist passengers with mobility challenges, including low floors for easy access and designated seating areas.

- Helpful Services:
    - If you require assistance, the bus drivers are typically helpful and can provide guidance.

5. Tourist Discounts and Passes

- Reykjavik City Card:
    - This card offers unlimited access to the public transport system,

along with free or discounted entry to various museums, attractions, and guided tours. It's a great option for travelers looking to maximize their experience in the city.

6. Alternative Public Transport Options

- Reykjavik Excursions:
  - In addition to Strætó, Reykjavik Excursions operates bus tours to popular tourist destinations outside the city, such as the Golden Circle and Blue Lagoon. These tours include transportation, making it easy to explore without the hassle of driving.

Car Rentals in Reykjavik: A Complete Guide

Renting a car in Reykjavik is one of the best ways to explore Iceland's stunning landscapes and natural wonders at your own pace. Here's everything you need to know about car rentals in Reykjavik:

1. Why Rent a Car in Reykjavik?

- Freedom and Flexibility:
  - Having a car allows you to explore not just Reykjavik, but also the stunning surrounding areas, such as the Golden Circle, South Coast, and beyond, without being tied to public transport schedules.

- Access to Remote Areas:
  - Some of Iceland's most beautiful attractions, like waterfalls, volcanoes, glaciers, and hot springs, are located in remote areas. Renting a car makes it easier to visit these spots, especially if you're interested in venturing off the beaten path.

2. Car Rental Companies

- Major Rental Agencies:
  - Reykjavik is home to many international car rental companies, including Hertz, Avis, Budget, and Europcar. These agencies typically have locations in both the city center and at Keflavik International Airport.

- Local Rental Agencies:
  - Local companies like Blue Car Rental, Reykjavik Cars, and SADcars often offer competitive pricing and good service. They specialize in vehicles suited to Iceland's terrain, including 4x4s for rugged routes.

- Airport vs. City Center Rentals:
  - You can pick up your rental car either at Keflavik International Airport upon arrival or in downtown Reykjavik. Airport rentals may be more convenient if you plan to start your road trip immediately.

3. Types of Vehicles Available

- Compact Cars:
  - Ideal for driving in Reykjavik and surrounding areas on paved roads. Compact cars are fuel-efficient and easier to park in the city.

- SUVs and 4x4s:
  - If you plan to drive in the highlands or on gravel roads (which are common in rural Iceland), renting a 4x4 is highly recommended. SUVs provide better control on rough terrain and in challenging weather conditions.

- Campervans:
  - For travelers looking to combine transportation and accommodation, campervans are a popular option. Iceland's numerous campsites make this an appealing way to explore the countryside.

4. Driving in Iceland: What to Know

- Road Conditions:
  - Roads in Reykjavik and along major tourist routes like the Golden Circle and Ring Road are well-maintained. However, some rural roads are gravel, and in the highlands, you'll encounter F-roads (mountain roads) that require a 4x4 vehicle.

- Weather Considerations:
  - Weather in Iceland can change rapidly, especially in winter, with conditions ranging from sunny skies to heavy snow or rain. It's

important to check the weather forecast and road conditions before setting out on a trip.

- Speed Limits:
    - The speed limit in urban areas like Reykjavik is usually 50 km/h (31 mph), while on rural roads, it's 90 km/h (56 mph). Always adhere to speed limits as traffic fines in Iceland are steep.

- Driving License Requirements:
    - Most rental companies require you to have a valid driving license from your home country, and you must be at least 20-25 years old (depending on the vehicle type) to rent a car.

- Fuel:
    - Gas stations are widely available around Reykjavik and along major routes. Most are self-service, and you can pay using credit or debit cards. Be aware that rural areas may have fewer fuel stops.

5. Insurance Options

- Basic Insurance:
    - Car rentals typically come with basic insurance, which includes Collision Damage Waiver (CDW) and Third-Party Liability coverage. However, this might not cover damage caused by gravel roads, sand, or ash storms.

- Additional Coverage:
    - It's advisable to add extra insurance options, such as:
    - Gravel Protection: For damage caused by loose gravel (common on

rural roads).

- Sand and Ash Protection: To cover potential damage from wind-blown ash or sand.

- Super CDW: Reduces your liability in case of accidents.

6. Cost of Renting a Car

- Pricing Factors:
  - Rental prices depend on the season (higher in summer), type of vehicle, and rental duration. It's often cheaper to book your rental car in advance, especially during peak tourist months.

- Fuel Costs:
  - Fuel is relatively expensive in Iceland, so factor this into your budget. Opting for a fuel-efficient vehicle can help reduce overall costs.

- Deposit and Payment:
  - Most rental companies require a credit card deposit, which is held as a security deposit for the duration of the rental. Be sure to check the company's policy before booking.

7. Parking in Reykjavik

- Paid Parking Zones:
  - Reykjavik has paid parking zones in the city center. You can pay at meters using cash or credit cards, or via mobile apps like "Reykjavik Parking."

- Free Parking:
   - Parking outside the city center is generally free, and some hotels offer complimentary parking for guests.

8. Tips for a Safe Road Trip

- Check the Weather and Road Conditions:
   - Always check the Icelandic Road and Coastal Administration website (www.road.is) for up-to-date road conditions and weather forecasts.

- Be Prepared for Narrow Bridges:
   - Many rural roads in Iceland have one-lane bridges, so be cautious and give way to oncoming traffic.

- Drive Carefully on Gravel Roads:
   - Slow down on gravel roads to avoid skidding or damaging your car, especially if you don't have gravel protection insurance.

- Be Mindful of Wildlife:
   - Sheep and other animals may wander onto the roads, particularly in rural areas. Drive carefully and remain alert.

Biking and Walking in Reykjavik: An Active Way to Explore

Reykjavik is a compact and walkable city, with plenty of bike-friendly routes that make it easy to get around on foot or by bike. Whether you're looking to explore the city center or venture into surrounding areas, here's a complete guide to biking and walking in Reykjavik:

1. Walking in Reykjavik

- Walkability:
  - Reykjavik is a pedestrian-friendly city, with many attractions located within easy walking distance of each other. The downtown area, known for its charming streets and vibrant culture, is perfect for leisurely strolls.

- Top Walkable Areas:
  - Laugavegur: Reykjavik's main shopping street, lined with boutiques, cafés, restaurants, and local shops.
  - Harpa to Sun Voyager: A scenic walk along Reykjavik's waterfront from Harpa Concert Hall to the Sun Voyager sculpture, offering stunning views of the sea and nearby mountains.
  - Austurvöllur Square: A central meeting spot surrounded by historical landmarks like the Reykjavik Cathedral and the Icelandic Parliament building.
  - Tjörnin Lake: A peaceful, picturesque walk around this downtown pond, where you can enjoy nature and bird-watching.

- City Walking Tours:
  - Reykjavik offers guided walking tours, focusing on history, culture, and local landmarks. These tours provide in-depth insights into the city's past, art scene, and architecture.

2. Biking in Reykjavik

- Cycling Culture:
  - Reykjavik is increasingly becoming a bike-friendly city, with designated bike paths and lanes, making cycling a great way to explore. The cool climate also makes biking a comfortable activity year-round, though wind and rain are common, so weather-appropriate gear is recommended.

- Bike Rentals:
  - Several companies in Reykjavik offer bike rentals, ranging from traditional bicycles to electric bikes. Popular rental spots include Reykjavik Bike Tours and Iceland Bike.
  - Rental shops often provide helmets, maps, and advice on the best cycling routes.

- Popular Biking Routes:
  - Reykjavik's Coastal Path: A popular cycling route that runs along the city's coastline, starting from downtown Reykjavik and extending out to Seltjarnarnes Peninsula. The path offers beautiful views of the ocean, mountains, and landmarks like Grotta Lighthouse.
  - Elliðaárdalur Valley: A nature reserve located just outside the city, offering a network of scenic cycling and walking paths alongside rivers, waterfalls, and lush greenery.

- Heiðmörk Nature Reserve: For those looking for a more challenging ride, this large wilderness area, located about 10 km outside the city, has trails for cycling through Iceland's striking landscapes of lava fields and forests.

- Reykjavik's Bike Paths:
  - The city has a well-marked network of bike paths, particularly along the waterfront and key arterial roads. These paths are separate from car traffic and provide a safe way to explore both urban and natural areas by bike.

3. Biking Tours

- Guided Bike Tours:
  - If you prefer exploring with a guide, Reykjavik offers various biking tours that cover different aspects of the city and its surroundings:
  - City Biking Tours: These tours take you through Reykjavik's neighborhoods and historical sites, offering insights into the city's culture and lifestyle.
  - Nature Biking Tours: Ideal for nature lovers, these tours guide cyclists through natural parks, coastal routes, and scenic viewpoints near Reykjavik.

- Electric Bike Tours:
  - For those looking to cover longer distances with less effort, electric bike tours are a popular option. These tours are perfect for exploring Reykjavik's outskirts or tackling longer routes like the Golden Circle without getting too tired.

4. Safety Tips for Walking and Biking

- Weather Considerations:
   - Iceland's weather is unpredictable, with frequent changes in wind, rain, and temperature. When walking or biking, always check the weather forecast and dress in layers to stay warm and dry.

- Footwear and Gear:
   - For walkers, comfortable, waterproof shoes are a must, especially if you're exploring nature areas. Cyclists should wear helmets, reflective gear, and bring a rain jacket in case of showers.

- Traffic Rules:
   - Bicycles share the road with cars in many parts of Reykjavik, so always follow Icelandic traffic laws. Cyclists should ride on the right side of the road, use hand signals, and yield to pedestrians on shared paths.

- Lighting and Visibility:
   - In winter, Reykjavik experiences limited daylight, so it's crucial to have reflective gear and lights for both biking and walking. Most rental bikes come with lights, but it's good to double-check.

5. Scenic Walks and Hikes Around Reykjavik

- Mount Esja:
   - Located just a 30-minute drive from Reykjavik, Mount Esja is a popular hiking destination offering breathtaking views of the city

and surrounding landscape. The hike has different levels of difficulty, making it suitable for both casual walkers and experienced hikers.

- Grotta Lighthouse:
    - A short walk or bike ride from downtown Reykjavik, Grotta Lighthouse is located on the tip of the Seltjarnarnes Peninsula. It's a peaceful spot, ideal for watching seabirds, the sunset, or the northern lights in winter.

- Öskjuhlíð Hill:
    - A forested area near the Perlan Museum, Öskjuhlíð offers walking trails with panoramic views of Reykjavik. It's a relaxing spot for an afternoon hike, and you can also visit the museum or enjoy the rotating restaurant at Perlan after your walk.

6. Biking and Walking Events

- Reykjavik Marathon:
    - Held annually in August, the Reykjavik Marathon offers participants the chance to run through the city's streets, alongside both locals and visitors. There are different race categories, including half-marathons and fun runs, for all fitness levels.

- Cycling Festivals:
    - Reykjavik occasionally hosts cycling events and festivals, celebrating sustainable transportation and outdoor activities. These are a great way to engage with the local biking community and explore new cycling routes.

Exploring Reykjavik

Historical and Cultural Landmarks in Reykjavik

Reykjavik, Iceland's capital and largest city, offers a rich blend of history, culture, and art. The city's landmarks reflect its unique heritage, from Viking roots to modern-day innovation. Below is a guide to the must-visit historical and cultural landmarks in Reykjavik:

1. Hallgrímskirkja Church

- Overview: The iconic Hallgrímskirkja is Reykjavik's most recognizable landmark, towering over the city with its striking, modernist architecture. The church is named after the Icelandic poet and clergyman Hallgrímur Pétursson and was designed by Guðjón Samúelsson, inspired by Iceland's basalt lava formations.
  - Highlights:
  - Observation Tower: Visitors can take an elevator to the top of the tower for breathtaking panoramic views of the city and surrounding landscapes.

- Leif Erikson Statue: In front of the church is a statue of Leif Erikson, the Norse explorer who is believed to have discovered America before Columbus.

2. National Museum of Iceland

- Overview: The National Museum offers an in-depth journey through Iceland's history, from its early settlement days to the modern era. Exhibits showcase artifacts, artworks, and manuscripts that tell the story of Iceland's culture and development.
    - Highlights:
    - Permanent Exhibition "Making of a Nation": A detailed display of Iceland's history, including Viking artifacts, medieval objects, and interactive installations.
    - Medieval Church Door: A famous wooden door from the 13th century, intricately carved with Christian motifs, is one of the museum's most prized artifacts.

3. Harpa Concert Hall and Conference Centre

- Overview: Harpa is a stunning modern architectural masterpiece on Reykjavik's waterfront. The building is known for its glass façade, designed to mimic the basalt landscapes of Iceland.
    - Cultural Significance:
    - Harpa is home to the Icelandic Symphony Orchestra and the Icelandic Opera, making it a key cultural hub for concerts, performances, and events.
    - The building itself is a visual landmark, particularly beautiful when lit up at night.

4. Reykjavik City Hall (Ráðhús Reykjavíkur)

- Overview: Located by Lake Tjörnin, Reykjavik City Hall is a modern, minimalist building that serves as the center of city administration.
  - Highlights:
  - 3D Map of Iceland: Inside the City Hall, visitors can see an impressive 3D map of Iceland, showcasing the country's geographical features.
  - Lake Tjörnin: The peaceful lake outside City Hall is a popular spot for bird-watching and relaxing walks.

5. The Settlement Exhibition – Reykjavík 871±2

- Overview: This fascinating archaeological museum is built around the remains of a Viking longhouse, dating back to the first settlers in Reykjavik around 871 AD.
  - Highlights:
  - The exhibit uses multimedia technology to bring the Viking Age to life, providing a glimpse into the daily lives of Iceland's first inhabitants.
  - Visitors can see original artifacts, such as tools and household items, and explore the interactive displays on Viking settlement.

6. Sun Voyager (Sólfar)

- Overview: The Sun Voyager is a striking steel sculpture located along Reykjavik's waterfront, symbolizing hope, progress, and the discovery of new horizons.
  - Cultural Significance: Designed by Jón Gunnar Árnason, the Sun Voyager is often interpreted as a Viking ship, connecting modern-day

Reykjavik with its seafaring past. It's also one of the most photographed landmarks in the city, particularly during sunset.

7. Perlan (The Pearl)

- Overview: Perlan is a unique glass-domed building situated on top of Öskjuhlíð Hill, offering panoramic views of Reykjavik and its surroundings. Originally built as water storage tanks, it has been transformed into a museum and exhibition space.
  - Highlights:
  - The Wonders of Iceland Exhibit: This exhibition includes a man-made ice cave, interactive displays about Iceland's glaciers, volcanoes, and geothermal activity.
  - The Observation Deck: Offers stunning 360-degree views of Reykjavik, the Atlantic Ocean, and nearby mountain ranges.

8. Árbæjarsafn (Reykjavik Open Air Museum)

- Overview: Árbæjarsafn is a living museum that preserves the heritage and lifestyle of Reykjavik's past. Visitors can explore historical buildings and homes from different periods, experiencing how Icelanders lived over the centuries.
  - Highlights:
  - Historical Houses: Many of the buildings have been relocated here from different parts of Reykjavik, including traditional turf houses and wooden homes from the 19th century.
  - Costumed Guides: The museum offers guided tours with staff dressed in period costumes, enhancing the historical experience.

9. The Icelandic Phallological Museum

- Overview: One of Reykjavik's more quirky cultural institutions, this museum is dedicated to the study of phallology, or the collection and display of penises from various species, including whales, seals, and even humans.
  - Cultural Significance: While humorous, the museum provides insights into Iceland's relationship with its natural environment and has become a must-see for visitors seeking something out of the ordinary.

10. Reykjavik Maritime Museum

- Overview: The Maritime Museum is located in the old harbor area and focuses on Iceland's rich fishing heritage, which has been a cornerstone of the nation's economy and culture for centuries.
  - Highlights:
    - Permanent Exhibition: "Fish & Folk – 150 Years of Fisheries" showcases the history of the Icelandic fishing industry, including its impact on Icelandic society and the nation's battle for control over its fishing grounds.
    - The Coast Guard Vessel Óðinn: Visitors can tour this historic ship, which played a key role in the Cod Wars between Iceland and the UK.

11. Höfði House

- Overview: Höfði House is a historic building in Reykjavik, famous for hosting the 1986 Reykjavik Summit, where Ronald Reagan and Mikhail Gorbachev met in a key moment of Cold War diplomacy.
  - Cultural Significance:

- Although not open to the public, the house is an important symbol of Reykjavik's role in global politics and diplomacy. Visitors can view the house from outside and read about its history on nearby plaques.

12. National Gallery of Iceland

- Overview: The National Gallery is Iceland's premier art museum, home to a wide range of Icelandic and international artworks, with a focus on 19th and 20th-century art.
 - Highlights:
 - The museum's collection features works by renowned Icelandic artists, such as Jóhannes S. Kjarval and Einar Jónsson, offering a glimpse into the nation's artistic heritage.

Hallgrímskirkja: The Iconic Landmark of Reykjavik

Overview

Hallgrímskirkja is one of Reykjavik's most recognizable and iconic landmarks. Standing 74.5 meters (244 feet) tall, this striking Lutheran church dominates the skyline of Iceland's capital city. Its unique architecture, inspired by Iceland's basalt lava formations, was designed by state architect Guðjón Samúelsson in 1937 and took over 40 years to complete, finally opening in 1986.

The church is named after the 17th-century clergyman and poet Hallgrímur Pétursson, best known for his collection of hymns, the "Passion Hymns" (Passíusálmar). It stands as a tribute to both his literary contribution and Iceland's religious heritage.

Architectural Significance

- Design Inspiration: Hallgrímskirkja's design was inspired by the hexagonal basalt columns formed by cooling lava, which are a common natural feature in Iceland. This gives the church its distinctively modern, yet naturalistic form, blending seamlessly with Iceland's volcanic landscape.
    - Exterior: The tower of Hallgrímskirkja rises like a modern interpretation of a Viking ship, symbolizing the country's strong seafaring heritage. The curved wings of the building give it an almost fortress-like appearance from afar.
    - Interior: The interior of the church is minimalist and serene, with tall, slender columns leading up to a high vaulted ceiling, creating a sense of space and tranquility. The focus is on simple forms and natural light that floods the space through large windows.

Must-See Features

- Observation Tower: One of the church's main attractions is the observation deck at the top of the tower. An elevator takes visitors up to stunning 360-degree views of Reykjavik and beyond. On clear days, you can see the colorful rooftops of the city, the Atlantic Ocean, and even the distant mountains and glaciers.
    - Leif Erikson Statue: Situated in front of Hallgrímskirkja is the statue of Leif Erikson, the Icelandic explorer believed to have discovered North America around 1000 AD, long before Columbus. The statue was a gift from the United States in 1930 to commemorate the 1,000th

anniversary of the Icelandic parliament, the Alþingi.

 - Organ: Inside the church, the large pipe organ is a key feature. Built by German organ builder Johannes Klais, it stands 15 meters tall and has 5,275 pipes. It is a significant instrument, frequently used for recitals and ceremonies, adding a majestic auditory element to the church's sacred space.

Visiting Hallgrímskirkja

- Location: Hallgrímskirkja is centrally located in Reykjavik and can be seen from almost anywhere in the city due to its towering height. It is a short walk from the main shopping street, Laugavegur.

 - Opening Hours: The church is open to visitors daily, though the tower closes earlier in the evening. Visitors should check the church's schedule for special events or services.

 - Entrance Fee: There is no fee to enter the main hall of the church, but a small fee is required to access the tower for the panoramic views.

Cultural Significance

Hallgrímskirkja is not only a place of worship but also a symbol of Reykjavik's cultural and religious identity. Its modern architecture reflects Iceland's unique natural environment and its connection to its past, particularly its Viking heritage and Christian faith. The church also serves as a venue for concerts and cultural events, further cementing its role as a community hub.

Harpa Concert Hall and Conference Centre: Reykjavik's Architectural Gem

Overview

Harpa Concert Hall and Conference Centre is one of Reykjavik's most remarkable modern landmarks, combining world-class acoustics with striking architecture. Opened in 2011, Harpa is a hub for Iceland's vibrant cultural scene, hosting concerts, operas, exhibitions, and conferences. Its glittering glass façade, inspired by Iceland's natural landscapes, makes it an iconic structure along the city's waterfront.

Designed by Danish firm Henning Larsen Architects in collaboration with Icelandic artist Ólafur Elíasson, Harpa is not only an important cultural venue but also a stunning architectural statement that reflects the dynamic and unpredictable nature of Iceland's environment.

Architectural Significance

- Glass Façade: The most distinctive feature of Harpa is its façade, composed of over 1,000 glass panels that change color with the shifting light and weather. These glass panels are inspired by Iceland's basalt rock formations and are arranged in a honeycomb pattern, creating a kaleidoscopic effect of light and color, especially when illuminated at night.
  - Location: Positioned right on Reykjavik's Old Harbor, Harpa offers stunning views of both the North Atlantic Ocean and Mount Esja. Its placement on the waterfront reflects the city's connection to both the

sea and the land, blending natural beauty with urban sophistication.

- Interior Design: Inside, Harpa's design emphasizes clean lines, open spaces, and natural light, offering a modern and airy atmosphere. The concert hall spaces themselves are designed to provide outstanding acoustics, ensuring an unparalleled experience for music lovers.

Must-See Features

- Eldborg Hall: The largest of Harpa's performance spaces, Eldborg (meaning "Fire Castle") is named after a volcanic crater and seats 1,800 people. Known for its excellent acoustics, this hall hosts the Iceland Symphony Orchestra, Icelandic Opera, and a variety of other large-scale performances, including international artists.

- Norðurljós and Silfurberg Halls: These smaller, versatile spaces are used for chamber music, conferences, and smaller performances. Norðurljós, meaning "Northern Lights," is named for its ethereal lighting that mimics the aurora borealis.

- Exhibitions and Events: In addition to concerts, Harpa regularly hosts art exhibitions, conferences, and cultural events, making it a lively center for creativity and innovation in Reykjavik. Harpa also offers free public events, such as performances by local musicians and exhibitions by Icelandic artists.

Visiting Harpa

- Location: Harpa is centrally located in downtown Reykjavik, within walking distance of the city's main attractions, including the old harbor, Laugavegur shopping street, and restaurants.

- Opening Hours: Harpa is open daily to the public, and visitors are welcome to explore the lobby, enjoy the views from the large windows, or take a guided tour of the concert hall spaces.

- Entrance Fees: There is no entrance fee to explore Harpa's public areas. However, tickets are required for concerts, performances, and events. Guided tours of the building are also available for a fee, providing visitors with deeper insight into the architecture and design of Harpa.

Cultural Significance

Harpa has quickly become a symbol of Iceland's cultural renaissance and innovation. It was constructed during a difficult economic period for Iceland, and its completion marked a turning point, symbolizing resilience and the country's commitment to arts and culture. Since opening, Harpa has become a venue for high-profile events, including the Reykjavik Arts Festival, the Iceland Airwaves Music Festival, and international conferences.

Harpa at Night

One of the most captivating times to visit Harpa is after sunset when its façade is illuminated with LED lights that dance and shift in different patterns. The ever-changing light show makes Harpa a true beacon of modern Reykjavik, drawing locals and tourists alike to admire its beauty against the backdrop of the night sky and harbor.

Dining and Shopping

- Restaurants and Cafes: Harpa houses several cafes and restaurants, offering a range of Icelandic cuisine with stunning views of the harbor. Visitors can enjoy a meal or coffee while taking in the atmosphere of one of Reykjavik's most scenic spots.

- Gift Shops: Harpa's shops feature unique Icelandic design and souvenirs, including handmade crafts, music, and books. Visitors can pick up one-of-a-kind Icelandic goods as a reminder of their trip to Reykjavik.

The National Museum of Iceland: Preserving Iceland's History and Heritage

Overview

The National Museum of Iceland (Þjóðminjasafn Íslands) is one of Reykjavik's most significant cultural institutions, dedicated to preserving and showcasing the history and heritage of Iceland from the settlement era to modern times. Founded in 1863, it has since amassed a vast collection of artifacts that offer an in-depth look into Icelandic life, culture, and history over the centuries.

The museum is located in a modern building close to the University of Iceland, making it easily accessible from the city center. It provides a comprehensive narrative of Iceland's journey through history, making it a must-visit for anyone interested in understanding the country's rich cultural and historical background.

Exhibitions and Displays

The National Museum's permanent exhibition, "Making of a Nation – Heritage and History in Iceland," takes visitors on a chronological journey through Iceland's past. The exhibition is divided into several sections, each exploring different periods and themes in Icelandic history, from the settlement era to the present day.

- Viking Settlement and Medieval Iceland: The early section focuses on the arrival of the Vikings in the 9th century, showcasing tools, weapons, and artifacts from the time. Highlights include ancient swords, religious artifacts, and the exhibition of a full-sized Viking boat.
  - The Saga Age and Christianity: The museum explores the transition of Iceland from paganism to Christianity around the year 1000, highlighting key artifacts like church relics, medieval manuscripts, and intricately carved religious icons. Visitors can learn about Iceland's Alþingi (parliament), one of the oldest functioning legislative bodies in the world, established in 930 AD.
  - The Danish Rule and Independence: A significant portion of the museum is devoted to Iceland's time under Danish rule and its journey toward independence in the early 20th century. Exhibits feature artifacts from this period, including furniture, clothing, and documents that illustrate Iceland's growing national consciousness.
  - Modern Iceland: The final sections of the exhibition deal with Iceland's modernization and its evolution in the 20th century. Visitors can explore exhibits related to the development of modern Icelandic society, with displays on urbanization, cultural life, and Iceland's growing role on the international stage.

Must-See Artifacts

- The Valþjófsstaður Door: One of the museum's most famous exhibits is a beautifully carved church door from the 13th century, known as the Valþjófsstaður Door. The intricate carvings on the door depict scenes from the legend of a knight and a lion and are a masterpiece of medieval Icelandic woodwork.

- Settlement-Era Artifacts: The museum has an impressive collection of Viking-age weapons, tools, and everyday objects that provide insight into the lives of Iceland's earliest settlers. Highlights include a well-preserved drinking horn, a Viking sword, and pieces of jewelry.

- Medieval Manuscripts: The National Museum holds rare and priceless medieval manuscripts, including sagas and legal texts that played a key role in preserving Iceland's history and literary heritage. These documents offer a glimpse into Iceland's strong literary tradition.

- Photography Collection: In addition to historical artifacts, the museum has an extensive photography collection that documents Icelandic life from the late 19th century to the present day, giving visitors a unique perspective on Iceland's transformation over time.

Special Exhibitions and Events

The National Museum also hosts temporary exhibitions that focus on various aspects of Icelandic culture and history, often exploring specific themes or artistic movements. These exhibitions change throughout the year, offering visitors something new to discover with each visit.

The museum also holds regular events, such as guided tours, lectures, and workshops that delve deeper into Iceland's history and cultural identity. These events often provide opportunities for hands-on learning and interaction with experts in the field.

Visitor Information

- Location: The museum is located near the University of Iceland, within walking distance of downtown Reykjavik. Its central location makes it a convenient stop during a day of exploring the city.
 - Opening Hours: The museum is open year-round, with extended hours in the summer months. Visitors should check the museum's website for current hours and any special holiday closings.
 - Entrance Fee: There is an admission fee to enter the National Museum, though children under 18 and certain other groups may enter for free. Admission includes access to all exhibitions and special events.
 - Audio Guides and Tours: The museum offers audio guides in multiple languages, providing detailed information about the exhibits. Visitors can also join guided tours led by knowledgeable staff to gain deeper insights into Iceland's history.

Cultural Significance

The National Museum of Iceland plays a crucial role in preserving and promoting Iceland's cultural heritage. It is not only a repository of Icelandic history but also a center for research and education, contributing to the country's national identity. By documenting the past and exploring contemporary culture, the museum helps visitors and locals alike understand the deep-rooted connections between Iceland's history and its modern society.

The Sun Voyager: Reykjavik's Symbol of Exploration and Dreams

Overview

The Sun Voyager (Sólfar in Icelandic) is one of Reykjavik's most iconic outdoor sculptures, located along the scenic waterfront, a short walk from the city center. Created by Icelandic artist Jón Gunnar Árnason, this striking steel structure was unveiled in 1990 as part of Reykjavik's 200th anniversary celebrations. While many associate it with a Viking ship, the Sun Voyager is more symbolic, representing a dream boat or an ode to the sun, embodying the themes of exploration, hope, freedom, and progress.

With its minimalist, skeletal frame facing out to the Atlantic Ocean, the Sun Voyager has become a beloved part of the Reykjavik landscape, attracting visitors for its beauty, symbolism, and the stunning backdrop it offers for photos.

Symbolism and Artistic Vision

- Dream Boat: The artist, Jón Gunnar Árnason, intended the sculpture to be a "dream boat" representing the desire for adventure, discovery, and the dream of uncharted territories. It was never meant to directly represent a Viking ship, though many see it as such, given Iceland's Viking heritage. Instead, it invites viewers to imagine the possibilities of travel, progress, and exploration of the unknown.
  - Connection to Nature: The Sun Voyager's design reflects Iceland's

intimate connection with the sea and the horizon. Positioned facing west, the sculpture catches the rays of the setting sun, creating a luminous, almost ethereal scene as sunlight glints off the polished steel, further enhancing its role as a tribute to the sun and a symbol of exploration.

 - Personal Journey: Árnason, who was terminally ill while designing the sculpture, also infused his work with a sense of personal journey, making the Sun Voyager not just a symbol of discovery, but a deeper, more personal reflection on life's voyage.

Location and Setting

 - Scenic Spot: The Sun Voyager sits on Reykjavik's Sæbraut promenade, along the waterfront, with panoramic views of Mount Esja in the background. On clear days, you can even catch glimpses of Snæfellsjökull glacier in the distance. The setting enhances the sculpture's meaning, blending the sculpture's aspirational theme with the vastness of the sea and sky.

 - Best Times to Visit: The sculpture is particularly breathtaking at sunrise and sunset, when the light creates dramatic reflections on the water and the polished steel structure. It's also a popular spot for photographers looking to capture the serenity and beauty of Reykjavik's coastal landscape.

Visiting the Sun Voyager

 - Accessibility: The Sun Voyager is easily accessible on foot from downtown Reykjavik. Many visitors enjoy taking a leisurely stroll along the scenic waterfront, which stretches from Harpa Concert Hall to Höfði House. The pathway is well-paved, making it suitable for walkers and cyclists.

- Free Attraction: Visiting the Sun Voyager is free of charge, making it a great addition to any Reykjavik itinerary. Its outdoor location also means it's open to visitors at any time of day or night.

Why It's a Must-Visit

- Photographic Beauty: The combination of the sculpture's sleek, minimalist design and its natural surroundings makes it a favorite spot for both amateur and professional photographers. The dramatic interplay between light, water, and steel creates endless photographic opportunities.

- Peaceful Reflection: The Sun Voyager is not just a place to take pictures; it's also a spot for quiet reflection. Many visitors find the sculpture and its setting to be a peaceful, contemplative space where they can sit, relax, and take in the expansive views of the ocean and the mountains beyond.

- Connection to Reykjavik's Spirit: The Sun Voyager represents Reykjavik's spirit of openness and progress, a city that celebrates its past but looks toward the future with optimism. The sculpture encapsulates the Icelandic values of exploration, resilience, and a deep connection to nature.

Reykjavik City Hall: A Blend of Modern Architecture and Civic Life

Overview

Reykjavik City Hall (Ráðhús Reykjavíkur) is not only the administrative hub of the city but also a striking example of modern architecture that blends harmoniously with its natural surroundings. Completed in 1992, the building sits on the northern shore of Tjörnin, Reykjavik's central lake, and serves as both a functional government space and a public gathering area. Its unique design and serene location make it a must-visit for architecture enthusiasts and those looking to explore the heart of Reykjavik's civic life.

The building is often celebrated for its seamless integration into the surrounding environment, with large windows that provide views of Tjörnin and the nearby birdlife, creating a peaceful atmosphere for both visitors and city officials alike.

Architecture and Design

- Contemporary Design: Designed by Icelandic architects Margrét Hardardóttir and Steve Christer, Reykjavik City Hall is a modernist building known for its clean lines, open spaces, and large, glass-paneled facades. The building is partly submerged in the lake, with walkways over the water that make it appear to float.
 - Integration with Nature: The architects intended to create a building that would blend with its environment, and this vision is evident in the way the building interacts with Tjörnin. The reflective water surface complements the minimalist design, while the structure itself provides an unobtrusive addition to Reykjavik's natural and urban landscape.
 - Accessible Space: Despite being a government building, City Hall is open to the public and invites citizens and tourists alike to explore its

interior, which includes exhibition spaces, a café, and an information center.

Must-See Features

- The 3D Map of Iceland: One of the highlights inside Reykjavik City Hall is the impressive 3D map of Iceland, which offers a detailed topographical view of the entire country. Visitors can walk around this large-scale model and gain a better understanding of Iceland's diverse geography, including its mountains, glaciers, volcanoes, and fjords. The map is an engaging educational tool and a favorite among visitors who want to visualize Iceland's rugged landscape.

- Exhibitions and Art Displays: The City Hall often hosts rotating exhibitions of contemporary Icelandic art, photography, and other cultural projects, making it not only a civic space but also a venue for artistic expression. These exhibitions give visitors insight into the vibrant local art scene.

- Public Spaces: The large atrium and public areas inside City Hall are filled with natural light, offering a welcoming and peaceful atmosphere. Visitors can sit by the large windows overlooking Tjörnin or visit the café for a drink while enjoying the calm surroundings.

The Importance of City Hall in Reykjavik

- Civic and Cultural Hub: While Reykjavik City Hall is a working government building, it also serves as a cultural and social hub for the city. It frequently hosts civic meetings, art exhibitions, and public events. Locals often visit City Hall to attend meetings or simply to enjoy its beautiful setting, making it an important gathering space for the

Reykjavik community.

- Environmental Sustainability: The building's design is environmentally conscious, featuring sustainable architectural practices and maximizing the use of natural light. This reflects Iceland's broader commitment to environmental sustainability and green living.

- A Symbol of Modern Reykjavik: Reykjavik City Hall is emblematic of the city's transformation from a quaint fishing town into a modern capital that balances tradition with progress. Its design is a statement of Reykjavik's forward-thinking attitude, all while maintaining a strong connection to nature.

Location and Access

- Central Location: Reykjavik City Hall is conveniently located in the heart of the city, adjacent to Tjörnin, a short walk from many of Reykjavik's key landmarks, including Austurvöllur Square, the Althingi (Parliament), and Laugavegur, the main shopping street.

- Walks Around Tjörnin: After visiting City Hall, visitors can enjoy a walk around Tjörnin Lake, where they can feed the ducks and swans, or simply take in the views of Reykjavik's colorful houses reflected on the water. The area around the lake is peaceful and ideal for a leisurely stroll, with several benches and paths to explore.

Visitor Information

- Opening Hours: Reykjavik City Hall is open to the public daily, with extended hours during the summer tourist season. Visitors are welcome to enter and explore the building's public areas.

- Free Admission: There is no entrance fee to visit City Hall, and the exhibitions and 3D map are available for all to enjoy.

- Café and Information Center: Inside the building, there is a café where visitors can relax and enjoy views of Tjörnin. The information center provides useful resources for tourists, including maps, brochures, and guidance on exploring Reykjavik and beyond.

Art and Entertainment in Reykjavik

Reykjavik, the cultural heart of Iceland, is a city that thrives on its vibrant arts and entertainment scene. From world-class galleries and museums to dynamic live music venues, the capital offers a diverse range of artistic expressions and entertainment options, making it a top destination for culture enthusiasts. Below is an extensive guide to the must-visit art and entertainment hotspots in Reykjavik.

1. Art Galleries and Museums

Reykjavik's art scene is a blend of the traditional and the contemporary, reflecting the city's rich history and its modern creative energy.

- The National Gallery of Iceland: This is the country's leading art museum, showcasing an impressive collection of 19th and 20th-century Icelandic art. The gallery also hosts temporary exhibitions of international artists, making it a hub for both local and global art.

- Reykjavik Art Museum: With three locations—Hafnarhús, Kjarvalsstaðir, and Ásmundarsafn—the Reykjavik Art Museum is the largest visual arts institution in Iceland. Each venue offers a unique focus: Hafnarhús presents contemporary exhibitions, Kjarvalsstaðir features works by the famous Icelandic artist Jóhannes S. Kjarval, and Ásmundarsafn is dedicated to the sculptor Ásmundur Sveinsson.

- The Living Art Museum (Nýló): This artist-run institution is a platform for experimental and avant-garde art. It features works from emerging and established Icelandic artists, as well as international creators pushing the boundaries of contemporary art.

- The Einar Jónsson Museum: Dedicated to Iceland's first sculptor, this museum houses an impressive collection of Einar Jónsson's works, ranging from large, dramatic sculptures to smaller, more intimate pieces. The sculpture garden outside is free to explore and offers a peaceful retreat in the heart of Reykjavik.

- The Icelandic Phallological Museum: One of the more eccentric attractions in Reykjavik, this museum is the only one of its kind in the world, showcasing an extensive collection of phallic specimens from various species. It's a quirky stop for those seeking something different in the city's art and culture scene.

2. Live Music and Concert Venues

Reykjavik is known for its thriving music scene, from indie rock to electronic beats, with numerous venues offering live performances throughout the week.

- Harpa Concert Hall and Conference Centre: Reykjavik's architectural gem, Harpa, is not only a stunning building but also a key venue for concerts, opera, and performances by the Iceland Symphony Orchestra and the Icelandic Opera. The glass facade, designed to reflect the Northern Lights, is worth visiting in itself, but the world-class acoustics inside make it a must for music lovers.

- Kaffibarinn: One of Reykjavik's most famous nightlife spots, Kaffibarinn is a small, cozy bar that regularly hosts live DJs and musicians. Known for its laid-back, bohemian atmosphere, it's a favorite among locals and tourists alike.

- Gaukurinn: This iconic venue is a hot spot for alternative music, comedy shows, and drag performances. Gaukurinn's eclectic programming ensures there's always something interesting happening, from rock bands to experimental electronic sets.

- Húrra: For fans of the Reykjavik underground music scene, Húrra offers a wide variety of live performances, ranging from punk to jazz. The intimate setting makes for a great night out, and its location in the downtown area means it's easy to include in a night of bar-hopping.

- Mengi: A venue and artist collective, Mengi is dedicated to experimental music and performance art. It's a must-visit for those seeking cutting-edge, avant-garde performances in Reykjavik's creative community.

3. Film and Theatres

Reykjavik also offers a variety of film and theatrical experiences, from mainstream cinema to indie screenings and live performances.

- Bio Paradis: Iceland's only art-house cinema, Bio Paradis is the place to go for independent films, Icelandic cinema, and foreign-language films. It's also home to various film festivals, including the Reykjavik International Film Festival (RIFF), which showcases the best in international and local filmmaking.

- National Theatre of Iceland: Founded in 1950, the National Theatre offers a range of performances, from classic Icelandic plays to contemporary international productions. Located in a striking building in central Reykjavik, it's a cultural hub for drama enthusiasts.

- Reykjavik City Theatre: This modern venue is known for its diverse programming, offering everything from musicals and classical plays to contemporary drama. With a strong focus on both Icelandic and international works, it's a key part of Reykjavik's theatre scene.

- Tjarnarbíó: An independent theatre and performance venue, Tjarnarbíó is home to some of the city's most innovative and experimental theatre productions. It often hosts productions by smaller theatre companies and emerging performers.

4. Festivals and Events

Reykjavik is home to several annual cultural events that celebrate art, music, and film, drawing international visitors.

- Reykjavik Arts Festival: Held annually in May, this festival is one of Iceland's premier cultural events. It features performances, exhibitions, and concerts by both Icelandic and international artists, covering a wide range of artistic disciplines.

- Airwaves Music Festival: Reykjavik Airwaves is one of the most famous music festivals in Iceland, showcasing both local and international bands across a variety of genres. It's a great way to experience Reykjavik's dynamic music scene, with performances happening in venues across the city.

- RIFF (Reykjavik International Film Festival): Every autumn, Reykjavik becomes a haven for film buffs during RIFF, which features screenings of cutting-edge films from around the world. The festival is known for its innovative programming and celebration of independent filmmaking.

- Culture Night (Menningarnótt): Held every August, Culture Night is a city-wide celebration of Reykjavik's art and culture, featuring free performances, exhibitions, and street parties. The event culminates in a spectacular fireworks display over the harbor.

5. Street Art and Urban Culture

Reykjavik's urban landscape is also home to a growing street art scene, with colorful murals and graffiti found throughout the city.

- Street Art in Downtown Reykjavik: A stroll through Reykjavik's downtown area will reveal numerous murals and artistic interventions, particularly in the neighborhoods of Laugavegur and Hlemmur. Local and international artists have contributed to the city's growing reputation as a hub for street art.

- Wall Poetry Project: One of the most famous street art initiatives in Reykjavik, Wall Poetry pairs street artists with musicians to create large-scale murals inspired by music. These pieces can be found scattered throughout the city, adding a layer of artistic expression to Reykjavik's urban environment.

Reykjavik Art Museum

The Reykjavik Art Museum (Listasafn Reykjavíkur) is the largest visual arts institution in Iceland and plays a significant role in the country's cultural landscape. With three main locations, the museum showcases a wide range of art, from traditional Icelandic works to contemporary pieces. Here's an in-depth look at what to expect when visiting the Reykjavik Art Museum.

Locations

1. Hafnarhús
  - Overview: Located by the harbor, Hafnarhús is the museum's main venue, renowned for its contemporary exhibitions. The building itself is a former fish-packing plant, which has been transformed into a vibrant art space.
  - Exhibitions: Hafnarhús features both permanent and temporary exhibitions, highlighting Icelandic artists and international contemporary art. The space regularly hosts solo exhibitions by notable artists, installation works, and multimedia presentations.
  - Facilities: The venue includes a café with beautiful views of the harbor, making it a perfect spot to relax after exploring the exhibits.

2. Kjarvalsstaðir

- Overview: This location is dedicated to the works of Jóhannes S. Kjarval, one of Iceland's most celebrated painters. Kjarvalsstaðir is surrounded by scenic parkland, enhancing the artistic experience.

 - Exhibitions: The museum showcases a large collection of Kjarval's works, emphasizing his unique approach to landscapes and the natural environment of Iceland. Temporary exhibitions often feature other Icelandic artists and themes related to nature and culture.

 - Architecture: The building's design, featuring large windows and open spaces, allows natural light to illuminate the artworks, creating an engaging atmosphere.

3. Ásmundarsafn

- Overview: Ásmundarsafn is dedicated to the works of sculptor Ásmundur Sveinsson, one of the pioneers of modern sculpture in Iceland. The museum is situated in a beautiful building that was once Sveinsson's home and studio.

 - Exhibitions: The collection includes many of Sveinsson's sculptures, drawings, and models, providing insight into his artistic process and contributions to Icelandic art. The museum also hosts temporary exhibitions by contemporary artists, often focusing on sculpture and installation art.

 - Sculpture Garden: The museum features an outdoor sculpture garden with many of Sveinsson's works, making it an inviting space for visitors to stroll and appreciate art in a natural setting.

Permanent Collection

The Reykjavik Art Museum's permanent collection includes a diverse range of works from Icelandic and international artists, highlighting various styles and movements. The museum's focus on contemporary art ensures that visitors can experience the dynamic nature of the current art scene. Key highlights of the collection include:

- Icelandic Art: The collection features significant works from Icelandic artists, capturing the country's unique cultural identity and landscape.
 - Contemporary Art: The museum showcases contemporary works that engage with current social, political, and environmental issues, reflecting the global art discourse.
 - Multimedia Installations: Many exhibitions incorporate new media and technology, allowing for immersive experiences that challenge traditional forms of art.

Special Exhibitions and Events

The Reykjavik Art Museum regularly hosts special exhibitions and events, providing opportunities for visitors to engage with the arts beyond the permanent collection. These may include:

- Artist Talks and Panels: Engage with artists and curators through discussions that delve into their creative processes and the themes explored in their work.
 - Workshops and Educational Programs: The museum offers workshops for all ages, encouraging hands-on exploration of art-making

techniques and concepts.

- Cultural Events: Throughout the year, the museum hosts cultural events, including performances, film screenings, and festivals that celebrate Icelandic culture and the arts.

Visitor Information

- Location: The Reykjavik Art Museum has three locations throughout the city, making it easily accessible for visitors.
- Opening Hours: Check the museum's official website for current opening hours and any changes due to holidays or special events.
- Admission: Entrance fees may vary by location; discounts are often available for students and seniors. Admission is typically free on specific days or during special events, so it's worth checking the schedule.
- Accessibility: The museum is committed to making art accessible to everyone, with facilities and programs designed for visitors with disabilities.

The Settlement Exhibition

The Settlement Exhibition is a fascinating cultural and historical attraction located in the heart of Reykjavik, Iceland. This exhibition provides visitors with an immersive experience that explores the Viking Age and the early settlement of Iceland. Here's a comprehensive overview of what to expect at the Settlement Exhibition:

Overview

- Purpose: The exhibition is designed to educate visitors about the history and archaeology of Iceland's early settlers, particularly focusing on the Viking period from the late 9th century onwards. It aims to present the origins of Reykjavik as one of the first inhabited areas in Iceland.
   - Location: Situated in a modern building on Aðalstræti, the exhibition is built around the remains of a Viking longhouse discovered during excavations in the early 2000s. The location itself is significant, as it is near where the first permanent settler, Ingólfur Arnarson, is believed to have landed.

Key Features

1. Archaeological Discoveries

- Excavated Remains: The exhibition prominently features the well-preserved ruins of a Viking longhouse, showcasing the architectural style and construction techniques of early Icelandic settlers. Visitors can walk around and view the remains, providing a direct connection to Iceland's past.
   - Artifacts: A variety of artifacts uncovered during the excavation are displayed, including tools, pottery, and everyday items that illustrate the daily lives of the early settlers.

2. Interactive Exhibits

- Multimedia Presentations: The exhibition incorporates modern technology, including interactive screens and audio-visual displays, to engage visitors. These elements provide in-depth information about Viking life, their customs, and the challenges they faced in settling in a harsh environment.
    - Reconstructed Environments: Visitors can experience recreated Viking settings, such as living quarters and communal spaces, giving them a tangible sense of how the early Icelanders lived and interacted.

3. Educational Programs

- Guided Tours: The Settlement Exhibition offers guided tours led by knowledgeable staff who provide detailed explanations of the exhibits, the historical context, and the significance of the findings.
    - Workshops and Activities: Occasionally, the exhibition hosts workshops aimed at families and school groups, providing hands-on experiences related to Viking history and culture.

Visitor Information

- Opening Hours: The Settlement Exhibition typically operates daily, but it is advisable to check the official website for current hours and any seasonal changes.
    - Admission: There is usually an entrance fee, with discounts available for students and seniors. Children under a certain age may have free entry.

- Accessibility: The exhibition is designed to be accessible to all visitors, with facilities for those with mobility challenges.
- Location: Its central location makes it easy to incorporate into a day of exploring Reykjavik's other attractions.

Laugavegur Street Shopping

Laugavegur is Reykjavik's main shopping street and one of the most vibrant areas in the city. Known for its eclectic mix of shops, boutiques, cafes, and cultural attractions, Laugavegur offers a unique shopping experience that reflects both local and international influences. Here's a comprehensive guide to shopping on Laugavegur Street:

Overview

- Length: Laugavegur stretches approximately 1.5 kilometers (about 1 mile) from Hlemmur Square to the city center, making it easy to explore on foot.
- Atmosphere: The street is lively, with a mix of locals and tourists, creating a bustling and friendly environment. It features colorful buildings, street art, and outdoor seating, especially during the summer months.

Shopping Highlights

1. Clothing and Fashion Boutiques

- Icelandic Design: Many shops focus on Icelandic fashion, offering unique clothing and accessories made from local materials. Look for wool sweaters (lopapeysa), stylish outerwear, and contemporary designs.
   - International Brands: In addition to local boutiques, you'll find popular international clothing brands, catering to a variety of tastes and styles.

2. Art and Craft Stores

- Local Artwork: Several galleries and shops showcase the work of Icelandic artists, including paintings, ceramics, and handcrafted jewelry. These make for great souvenirs and gifts.
   - Handicrafts: Look for shops offering traditional Icelandic handicrafts, such as woolen goods, pottery, and unique home decor items.

3. Souvenir Shops

- Icelandic Souvenirs: Numerous stores sell a variety of souvenirs, from traditional items like Viking helmets and miniature trolls to modern keepsakes that reflect Icelandic culture and nature.
   - Eco-Friendly Products: Many shops emphasize sustainability and eco-friendliness, offering products made from natural materials or promoting responsible tourism.

4. Bookstores and Music Shops

- Local Literature: Discover Icelandic literature, including novels, poetry, and books on Icelandic history and culture. English translations are often available.
　- Music: Some shops specialize in Icelandic music, featuring local artists and bands. Vinyl records and CDs make great gifts for music lovers.

5. Food and Specialty Stores

- Gourmet Foods: Explore shops that offer Icelandic delicacies such as dried fish, licorice, and local honey. Many stores also carry specialty chocolates and organic products.
　- Cafes and Bakeries: Laugavegur is home to cozy cafes and bakeries where you can take a break and enjoy traditional Icelandic pastries like kleinur (twisted doughnuts) or a slice of cake.

Dining and Refreshments

- Cafes and Restaurants: Alongside shopping, Laugavegur boasts a variety of dining options, ranging from casual eateries to upscale restaurants. Many places offer outdoor seating, perfect for people-watching.
　- Street Food: Look for food stalls or small vendors selling Icelandic street food, including hot dogs (pylsur) and traditional fish dishes, ideal for a quick snack while exploring.

Cultural Attractions

- Art Galleries: In addition to shopping, Laugavegur is home to several art galleries that feature contemporary Icelandic art. Consider stopping by to appreciate local talent.
  - Street Art: The area is known for its vibrant street art and murals, adding to the artistic atmosphere of the street. Take time to explore and photograph these colorful displays.

Tips for Shopping on Laugavegur

- Opening Hours: Most shops on Laugavegur are open from 10 AM to 6 PM, with some staying open later on weekends. However, it's good to check individual store hours.
  - Payment Options: Credit and debit cards are widely accepted in Iceland, making it convenient to shop without carrying large amounts of cash.
  - Sales Tax: Prices in Iceland include VAT, and tourists can claim a tax refund on certain purchases if they spend over a specific amount.
  - Sustainable Shopping: Many shops on Laugavegur focus on sustainable practices, so consider supporting local artisans and eco-friendly products.

Nightlife and Live Music Venues in Reykjavik

Reykjavik's nightlife is vibrant and diverse, offering a range of options for all tastes. The city comes alive after dark with a mix of cozy bars, energetic nightclubs, and intimate live music venues. Whether you're looking to enjoy a quiet drink, dance the night away, or experience local music, Reykjavik has something for everyone. Here's a comprehensive guide to the nightlife and live music scene in Reykjavik:

Overview of Reykjavik's Nightlife

- Late-Night Culture: Reykjavik's nightlife typically begins late, with bars and clubs filling up after 10 PM. Many venues stay open until the early hours, especially on weekends.
  - Safety and Atmosphere: The city is known for its friendly and safe atmosphere, making it easy for locals and visitors to socialize and enjoy the nightlife.

Popular Nightlife Areas

1. **Laugavegur Street:** The main shopping street transforms into a nightlife hub with numerous bars, clubs, and restaurants. It's the perfect place to start your night.
2. **Hlemmur Square:** This area features trendy bars and eateries, offering a lively ambiance and a mix of locals and tourists.
3. **Grandi Harbor Area:** Known for its relaxed vibe, this waterfront

area has unique bars and eateries with scenic views of the harbor.

Bars and Pubs

1. Micro Bar:

- Description: A cozy bar specializing in Icelandic craft beers and a rotating selection of local brews. The laid-back atmosphere is perfect for enjoying a casual drink.
    - Highlights: Friendly staff, a great selection of beers on tap, and a warm, welcoming vibe.

2. Pablo Discobar:

- Description: A fun and colorful bar with a Latin twist, featuring cocktails, dancing, and a vibrant atmosphere.
    - Highlights: Regular themed nights, including salsa and reggaeton.

3. The English Pub:

- Description: A popular pub with a traditional British vibe, offering a wide selection of beers and comfort food.
    - Highlights: Sports screenings, trivia nights, and a lively crowd.

4. Kaffibarinn:

- Description: A legendary bar known for its eclectic decor and laid-back atmosphere, often featuring live music.
    - Highlights: A mix of locals and tourists, excellent cocktails, and a welcoming vibe.

Nightclubs

1. Paloma:

- Description: One of Reykjavik's most popular nightclubs, known for its eclectic music selection, ranging from electronic to hip-hop.
    - Highlights: Regular themed parties, a spacious dance floor, and a vibrant atmosphere.

2. Sirkus:

- Description: A lively nightclub that often hosts live DJs and themed dance parties.
    - Highlights: A diverse crowd and a fun, energetic vibe make it a favorite among locals.

3. Rauðka:

- Description: Known for its unique decor and laid-back vibe, Rauðka features local DJs and a fun dance atmosphere.
  - Highlights: A mix of music genres and a friendly crowd.

Live Music Venues

1. Harpa Concert Hall:

- Description: A stunning architectural landmark hosting a variety of performances, from classical concerts to contemporary music events.
  - Highlights: Check their schedule for performances by local and international artists.

2. Gaukurinn:

- Description: A popular venue for live music, offering a diverse lineup of bands and genres, from rock to folk.
  - Highlights: Karaoke nights, trivia, and open mic events, in addition to regular concerts.

3. Húrra:

- Description: A lively venue featuring local and international bands across various genres, including rock, jazz, and electronic.
  - Highlights: A great place to discover up-and-coming artists and

enjoy themed nights.

4. Bravó:

- Description: A smaller venue known for hosting intimate live music performances and jam sessions.
    - Highlights: A relaxed atmosphere, perfect for enjoying local talent.

5. Harbor House:

- Description: A cultural venue that often hosts folk music, traditional Icelandic music, and more contemporary performances.
    - Highlights: The scenic views of the harbor add to the experience.

Tips for Enjoying Reykjavik's Nightlife

- Plan Ahead: Check the schedules of live music venues and bars for any special events or performances. Many venues have websites or social media pages with updated information.
    - Dress Code: While Reykjavik is relatively casual, some clubs may have a dress code. Smart casual attire is usually a safe choice.
    - Transportation: Reykjavik is walkable, but if you venture further out, consider using taxis or rideshare services. Public transportation is limited late at night.
    - Respect Local Customs: Drinking culture in Iceland is generally relaxed, but it's essential to be respectful and considerate of others, especially in quieter venues.

Outdoor Activities in Reykjavik

Hiking and Nature Walks in Reykjavik

Reykjavik is not only the capital of Iceland but also a gateway to breathtaking natural landscapes, making it an ideal base for hiking and nature walks. With its stunning scenery, diverse terrain, and proximity to various natural attractions, there are countless opportunities to explore the great outdoors. Here's a comprehensive guide to hiking and nature walks in and around Reykjavik.

Overview of Hiking in Reykjavik

- Accessibility: Many hiking trails are easily accessible from the city, making it convenient for both novice and experienced hikers to explore.
    - Diversity: The trails vary in difficulty, from leisurely walks suitable for families to challenging hikes for seasoned adventurers.
    - Natural Beauty: Hikers can expect to see stunning landscapes, including mountains, valleys, geothermal areas, and coastal views.

Popular Hiking Trails and Nature Walks

1. Esjan (Mount Esja)

- Difficulty: Moderate to Challenging
  - Distance: Varies (up to 10 km round trip)
  - Duration: 2 to 4 hours
  - Highlights:
  - Mount Esja is a popular hiking destination just a short drive from Reykjavik, offering stunning views of the city and surrounding landscapes.
  - The main trail leads to a viewpoint called "Steinn" or continues to the summit for more experienced hikers.
  - Enjoy panoramic views of Reykjavik, Faxaflói Bay, and the Snæfellsnes Peninsula on a clear day.

2. Heiðmörk Nature Reserve

- Difficulty: Easy to Moderate
  - Distance: Various trails (up to 20 km total)
  - Duration: 1 to 3 hours
  - Highlights:
  - Located within Reykjavik's city limits, Heiðmörk offers several well-marked trails through birch forests, lava fields, and around small lakes.
  - It's an excellent spot for birdwatching and enjoying local flora and fauna.
  - Trails like "Múlagljúfur" provide beautiful views of the surrounding landscape and are suitable for families.

3. Glymur Waterfall

- Difficulty: Moderate
    - Distance: Approximately 7 km (round trip)
    - Duration: 2 to 3 hours
    - Highlights:
    - Glymur is one of Iceland's tallest waterfalls, located in the Hvalfjörður fjord area, about a 1-hour drive from Reykjavik.
    - The hike to the waterfall involves some steep sections and river crossings but rewards hikers with stunning views of the waterfall and surrounding mountains.
    - The trail provides opportunities to see diverse landscapes, including moss-covered rocks and unique geological formations.

4. Reykjavik Coastal Path

- Difficulty: Easy
    - Distance: Approximately 5 km (one way)
    - Duration: 1 to 2 hours
    - Highlights:
    - This scenic coastal path runs along the waterfront from Harpa Concert Hall to the suburb of Nauthólsvík.
    - Enjoy views of the ocean, mountains, and the city's skyline while walking or biking.
    - The path is accessible year-round and is suitable for all fitness levels, making it perfect for families and casual walkers.

5. Þingvellir National Park

- Difficulty: Easy to Moderate
  - Distance: Varies (up to 15 km on different trails)
  - Duration: 2 to 4 hours
  - Highlights:
- A UNESCO World Heritage Site located about 45 minutes from Reykjavik, Þingvellir is famous for its geological and historical significance.
- The park features various trails that take you through stunning landscapes, including rift valleys, lakes, and historical sites.
- Don't miss the Öxarárfoss waterfall and the Silfra fissure, where you can see the divide between the North American and Eurasian tectonic plates.

6. Mount Keilir

- Difficulty: Moderate
  - Distance: Approximately 8 km (round trip)
  - Duration: 2 to 3 hours
  - Highlights:
- Located near the Blue Lagoon, Mount Keilir offers a relatively short but steep hike to its summit, providing incredible views of the Reykjanes Peninsula and the surrounding area.
- The trail is well-marked, and hikers can enjoy unique volcanic landscapes along the way.

OUTDOOR ACTIVITIES IN REYKJAVIK

Tips for Hiking and Nature Walks in Reykjavik

- Weather Preparedness: Icelandic weather can be unpredictable. Dress in layers, wear waterproof clothing, and check the weather forecast before heading out.

  - Footwear: Wear sturdy hiking boots or shoes with good grip, especially for trails with uneven terrain or steep sections.

  - Stay Hydrated: Bring plenty of water, especially for longer hikes, and pack snacks to keep your energy up.

  - Leave No Trace: Respect the environment by staying on marked trails and following Leave No Trace principles to preserve Iceland's natural beauty.

  - Guided Tours: If you're unsure about hiking alone or want to explore more remote areas, consider joining a guided hiking tour. Local guides can provide valuable insights into the landscape, flora, and fauna.

Mount Esja: A Comprehensive Guide

Overview of Mount Esja

Mount Esja (Esjan) is a prominent mountain range located just north of Reykjavik, Iceland. It stands at 914 meters (2,999 feet) and is a popular destination for both locals and tourists seeking outdoor adventure. Known for its stunning views, diverse hiking trails, and geological significance, Mount Esja is an essential part of the Reykjavik landscape and offers a unique experience for hikers of all skill levels.

Getting There

- Location: Mount Esja is located approximately 10 kilometers (6 miles) from downtown Reykjavik.
  - Transportation:
  - Car: The easiest way to reach Mount Esja is by car. There is parking available at the Esja Nature Reserve parking lot, which serves as the starting point for most trails.
  - Public Transport: Take bus number 15 from the city center to the "Esjuhlíð" stop, followed by a short walk to the trailhead.

Hiking Trails

Mount Esja features several well-marked hiking trails that cater to different levels of experience. Here are some of the most popular routes:

1. The Main Trail to Steinn

- Difficulty: Moderate
  - Distance: Approximately 4 kilometers (2.5 miles) one way
  - Duration: 1.5 to 2 hours one way
  - Highlights:
  - This trail leads to a viewpoint known as "Steinn," offering panoramic views of Reykjavik, Faxaflói Bay, and the surrounding mountains.
  - The trail is relatively well-maintained, with some steep sections, making it suitable for those with moderate fitness levels.
  - The ascent provides opportunities to see unique geological forma-

tions and diverse vegetation.

2. The Summit Trail (Esjan Summit)

- Difficulty: Challenging
    - Distance: Approximately 7 kilometers (4.3 miles) round trip
    - Duration: 4 to 5 hours
    - Highlights:
    - For experienced hikers, this trail continues from Steinn to the summit of Mount Esja.
    - The trail becomes steeper and more rugged, requiring good physical fitness and appropriate gear.
    - The summit offers breathtaking views of the surrounding landscape and is a rewarding achievement for those who reach it.

3. Búrfell Trail

- Difficulty: Easy to Moderate
    - Distance: Approximately 6 kilometers (3.7 miles) round trip
    - Duration: 2 to 3 hours
    - Highlights:
    - This trail is less crowded and provides a more tranquil hiking experience.
    - The path winds through picturesque landscapes, including lava fields and birch forests, making it a great option for families and casual walkers.

What to Expect

- Scenic Views: Mount Esja offers some of the best views in the area. On clear days, hikers can see the Snaefellsnes Peninsula, the Reykjanes Peninsula, and even the Westfjords.
  - Diverse Flora and Fauna: The area is home to a variety of plant species, birds, and other wildlife. Keep an eye out for puffins and other seabirds along the coastal cliffs.
  - Changing Weather: Be prepared for rapidly changing weather conditions. It's not uncommon to experience sun, rain, and wind all in one hike. Always check the weather forecast before heading out.
  - Photography Opportunities: The dramatic landscapes and unique geological features make Mount Esja a fantastic location for photography, especially at sunrise and sunset.

Tips for Hiking Mount Esja

- Dress Appropriately: Wear layers and bring waterproof clothing, as the weather can change quickly. Sturdy hiking boots are essential for navigating the rugged terrain.
  - Bring Essentials: Carry enough water, snacks, and a first-aid kit. A fully charged mobile phone can be helpful for navigation and emergencies.
  - Respect Nature: Stay on marked trails to protect the environment and avoid damaging the delicate vegetation. Follow Leave No Trace principles to preserve the natural beauty of Mount Esja.
  - Plan Your Hike: Start your hike early in the day to allow plenty of time to complete your journey and enjoy the views. Check trail

conditions, especially in winter, as some paths may be icy or snow-covered.

Heiðmörk Nature Reserve: A Comprehensive Guide

Overview of Heiðmörk Nature Reserve

Heiðmörk Nature Reserve is a stunning natural area located just a short distance from Reykjavik, Iceland. Covering approximately 3,000 hectares, it is characterized by diverse landscapes, including birch forests, lava fields, lakes, and geothermal areas. Heiðmörk is a favorite spot for locals and tourists alike, offering a range of outdoor activities such as hiking, cycling, and birdwatching.

Getting There

- Location: Heiðmörk is situated about 10 kilometers (6 miles) from downtown Reykjavik.
  - Transportation:
  - Car: The easiest way to reach the reserve is by car, with parking available at several trailheads within the park.
  - Public Transport: You can take bus number 6 from the city center to the "Víðimýr" stop, followed by a short walk to the reserve entrance.

Activities in Heiðmörk

Heiðmörk offers a variety of outdoor activities suitable for all ages and fitness levels. Here are some of the most popular activities:

1. Hiking

- Trail Variety: Heiðmörk features an extensive network of hiking trails ranging from easy walks to more challenging routes.
  - Popular Trails:
  - Bergsholt Trail: A relatively easy trail that winds through beautiful birch forests, offering a peaceful hiking experience.
  - Vallaskógur Trail: A moderate trail that leads to scenic viewpoints and offers opportunities to explore the unique flora and fauna of the area.
  - Laugarás Trail: A longer route that takes you around the stunning lakes in the reserve, perfect for a full-day hike.

2. Cycling

- Bike-Friendly Paths: Heiðmörk has numerous well-maintained paths suitable for cycling, making it a great destination for bike enthusiasts.
  - Mountain Biking: For more adventurous cyclists, there are challenging trails that navigate through the rugged terrain and diverse landscapes.

3. Birdwatching

- Diverse Wildlife: Heiðmörk is home to various bird species, making it a prime spot for birdwatching. Look for ducks, geese, and various migratory birds, especially during the spring and summer months.

4. Fishing

- Fishing Opportunities: Several lakes in Heiðmörk are stocked with trout, making it a popular destination for fishing enthusiasts.
    - Fishing Licenses: Ensure you obtain the necessary fishing licenses, which can typically be purchased at local shops or online.

5. Picnicking

- Scenic Picnic Areas: There are designated picnic spots throughout the reserve, perfect for enjoying a meal surrounded by nature.
    - Facilities: Some areas have tables and benches, but it's advisable to bring your own supplies.

Flora and Fauna

Heiðmörk is known for its rich biodiversity, showcasing a unique blend of native Icelandic plants and imported species. Key highlights include:

- Vegetation: The reserve features lush birch forests, colorful wildflowers, and various shrubs. In addition, you can find moss-covered lava fields and geothermal areas.

- Wildlife: Besides birds, you may spot various mammals, such as Arctic foxes, rabbits, and reindeer, as well as numerous insects and butterflies during the warmer months.

Tips for Visiting Heiðmörk

- Dress in Layers: Weather conditions can change rapidly in Iceland. Dress in layers and wear waterproof clothing to stay comfortable.

- Stay Hydrated: Bring plenty of water, especially if you plan on hiking or cycling for an extended period.

- Respect Nature: Follow Leave No Trace principles by staying on marked trails and not disturbing wildlife or vegetation.

- Check Trail Conditions: In winter, some trails may be icy or snow-covered. Ensure you have appropriate gear and check local conditions before heading out.

Viðey Island: A Comprehensive Guide

Overview of Viðey Island

Viðey Island, located just off the coast of Reykjavik, is a serene and beautiful destination known for its natural beauty, historical significance, and cultural heritage. The island covers about 1.7 square kilometers (0.66 square miles) and is a popular spot for both locals and tourists seeking a peaceful escape from the bustling city. With stunning landscapes, walking paths, and unique art installations, Viðey offers a unique experience for outdoor enthusiasts and history buffs alike.

Getting There

- Location: Viðey Island is situated approximately 2.5 kilometers (1.6 miles) from Reykjavik's old harbor.
    - Transportation:
    - Ferry: The most common way to reach the island is by taking a ferry operated by the Viðey Ferry. The ferry departs regularly from the Old Harbor in Reykjavik and takes about 15-20 minutes to reach the island.
    - Tickets: Tickets can be purchased at the ferry terminal or online in advance.
    - Operating Hours: Ferry services may vary by season, so checking the schedule ahead of your visit is advisable.

Attractions on Viðey Island

1. Walking and Biking Trails

- Nature Trails: Viðey is home to several well-marked walking and biking paths that wind through the island's diverse landscapes, including coastal areas, grassy hills, and scenic viewpoints.
    - Scenic Views: The trails offer stunning views of Reykjavik, the surrounding mountains, and the nearby Faxaflói Bay.

2. Viðey House (Viðeyjarstofa)

- Historical Significance: Built in the 18th century, Viðey House is one of the oldest buildings in Iceland. It served as a summer residence for wealthy families and is now a café and exhibition space.
  - Café and Events: Visitors can enjoy refreshments at the café while taking in the beautiful surroundings. The house also hosts cultural events and exhibitions throughout the year.

3. The Imagine Peace Tower

- Art Installation: Created by Yoko Ono in memory of John Lennon, the Imagine Peace Tower is a unique light installation that shines upward into the sky. It is located on Viðey Island and is best viewed from late September to early October.
  - Symbol of Peace: The installation serves as a symbol of peace and is meant to inspire visitors to promote global harmony. A plaque featuring Lennon's famous quote "Imagine all the people living life in peace" is also located near the tower.

4. Historic Ruins and Structures

- Old Buildings and Monuments: Throughout the island, visitors can explore the remains of old structures, including ruins of old farms and churches that reflect the island's rich history.
  - Sculptures: Various sculptures and art installations are scattered around the island, adding a cultural touch to the natural landscape.

5. Birdwatching and Wildlife

- Diverse Birdlife: Viðey Island is an excellent location for birdwatching, especially during spring and summer when various migratory birds nest on the island. Common sightings include puffins, eider ducks, and Arctic terns.
   - Nature and Flora: The island's varied ecosystems support different plant species, offering a picturesque setting for nature enthusiasts.

Tips for Visiting Viðey Island

- Plan Your Visit: Check the ferry schedule ahead of time, especially during off-peak seasons, to ensure you have enough time to explore the island.
   - Dress for the Weather: Weather in Iceland can be unpredictable, so wear layers and be prepared for wind and rain, even in summer.
   - Bring Snacks and Water: While there are facilities available, bringing your own refreshments can enhance your experience, especially if you plan to hike or explore for an extended time.
   - Respect Nature: Follow the marked paths and guidelines to protect the island's natural beauty and wildlife.

Whale Watching in Reykjavik: A Comprehensive Guide

Overview of Whale Watching in Reykjavik

Reykjavik is one of the best places in the world for whale watching, thanks to its unique geographic location and rich marine biodiversity. The waters surrounding Iceland, particularly in the Faxaflói Bay, are home to various whale species, including humpback whales, minke whales, orcas, and even the majestic blue whale. Whale watching tours provide a thrilling opportunity to observe these magnificent creatures in their natural habitat while enjoying the breathtaking Icelandic scenery.

Best Time for Whale Watching

- Peak Season: The best time for whale watching in Reykjavik is from May to September, when the waters are warmer, and the whales are more active.
    - May to August: Humpback whales are commonly seen during these months.
    - June to September: Minke whales, orcas, and other species are often spotted during this time.
    - Winter Tours: While winter is not peak season, some tours operate, primarily focusing on orcas, especially around Snæfellsnes Peninsula.

Types of Whale Watching Tours

1. Boat Tours

- Traditional Whale Watching Boats: Most tours are conducted on large, stable boats designed for comfort and safety. These tours typically last 2-3 hours.
  - Luxury Yachts: For a more upscale experience, consider a luxury yacht tour, which may offer gourmet food, drinks, and fewer passengers for a more intimate experience.
  - RIB Boat Tours: For the adventurous, RIB (rigid inflatable boat) tours provide a faster and more exhilarating way to search for whales. These tours can cover more area in less time and often allow for closer encounters.

2. Kayaking Tours

- Eco-Friendly Experience: Kayaking tours offer a unique and intimate way to observe whales and marine life. Paddling in small groups allows for quieter exploration of the waters, increasing the chances of sightings.
  - Guided Tours: Experienced guides lead these tours, providing insights into the marine ecosystem and ensuring safety.

3. Sightseeing Cruises

- Combination Tours: Some tours combine whale watching with sightseeing, allowing you to explore the stunning coastal landscapes, including islands like Viðey and Grótta.
  - Food and Drink Options: Certain cruises offer on-board dining options, making it a relaxing experience to enjoy a meal while searching for whales.

What to Expect on a Whale Watching Tour

- Whale Species: Depending on the time of year, you may encounter various species, including:
    - Humpback Whales: Known for their acrobatics, they are often seen breaching and flapping their fins.
    - Minke Whales: The smallest baleen whale, recognizable by its sleek shape.
    - Orcas: These social animals are often spotted in pods and are known for their striking black-and-white coloring.
    - Blue Whales: The largest animals on Earth can be spotted in deeper waters, particularly during summer.

- Wildlife Sightings: In addition to whales, you might also see dolphins, puffins, seabirds, and various marine life.

- Expert Guides: Knowledgeable guides accompany the tours to share fascinating facts about the whales, their behavior, and the surrounding ecosystem.

What to Bring

- Clothing: Dress in layers, as temperatures on the water can be significantly cooler than on land. Waterproof clothing and windbreakers are recommended.
    - Footwear: Wear sturdy, non-slip shoes for safety on the boat.
    - Camera: Bring a camera or smartphone to capture the incredible sights, but also be mindful of your surroundings and fellow passengers.

- Binoculars: While many tours offer good viewing spots, binoculars can enhance your whale-watching experience.
- Sunscreen: Even on cloudy days, UV rays can reflect off the water, so apply sunscreen to protect your skin.

Tips for a Successful Whale Watching Experience

- Arrive Early: Arrive at the harbor early to ensure a good seat and to check in on time.
- Stay Patient: Whale watching can be unpredictable; sometimes it takes a while to spot a whale, so be patient and enjoy the scenery in the meantime.
- Respect Wildlife: Follow guidelines set by the tour operators and respect the animals' space.

Here's a list of some of the best whale watching tours in Reykjavik, highlighting their features, duration, and unique offerings:

1. Elding Whale Watching

- Tour Type: Traditional Boat Tour
    - Duration: 2.5 to 3 hours
    - Highlights:
    - Offers a variety of tours, including family-friendly options.
    - Equipped with indoor and outdoor viewing areas.
    - Experienced guides provide information on whale species and marine life.
    - Sightings include humpback whales, minke whales, orcas, and dolphins.
    - Extras: Complimentary hot chocolate and snacks are available on board.

2. Special Tours

- Tour Type: Small Group Tours (RIB Boat)
    - Duration: 2 hours
    - Highlights:
    - Offers a thrilling experience on fast RIB boats that can reach whales quickly.
    - Maximum of 12 passengers for an intimate experience.
    - Opportunity to see a variety of whales and dolphins, with great chances of close encounters.

- Guides share detailed information about the local wildlife and the ecosystem.
 - Extras: Provided with waterproof suits for comfort.

3. Whale Safari

- Tour Type: Traditional and RIB Boat Tours
 - Duration: 3 hours for traditional tours; 2 hours for RIB tours.
 - Highlights:
 - Operates both large and small boat tours, catering to different preferences.
 - Offers a "Whale Watching Guarantee" - if you don't see a whale, you can join again for free.
 - Experienced guides with in-depth knowledge of marine biology.
 - Extras: Onboard café with snacks and drinks available for purchase.

4. Reykjavik Sailors

- Tour Type: Traditional Boat Tour
 - Duration: 2.5 to 3 hours
 - Highlights:
 - Focuses on small group sizes for a more personal experience.
 - Offers a relaxed atmosphere with knowledgeable guides.
 - Tours include educational talks about the whales and conservation efforts.
 - Extras: Free hot drinks and warm overalls provided on board.

5. Sailing Reykjavik

- Tour Type: Sailing Tour on a Yacht
  - Duration: 2.5 to 3 hours
  - Highlights:
  - Experience whale watching from a sailing yacht, providing a unique perspective and quieter exploration.
  - Small group size for a more exclusive experience.
  - Enjoy refreshments on board while sailing through Faxaflói Bay.
  - Extras: Comfortable seating and an eco-friendly approach to whale watching.

6. Eagle Eye Tours

- Tour Type: Private Whale Watching Tours
  - Duration: Customizable
  - Highlights:
  - Offers personalized tours for families or groups, ensuring a tailored experience.
  - Combines whale watching with sightseeing opportunities, such as visiting nearby islands.
  - The opportunity for custom itineraries based on your interests.
  - Extras: Snacks and drinks provided during the tour.

7. Fjordsafari

- Tour Type: Combo Whale Watching and Fjord Exploration
  - Duration: 3 to 4 hours
  - Highlights:

- Combines whale watching with a scenic tour of the stunning fjords surrounding Reykjavik.

- Includes knowledgeable guides sharing insights about the geography and wildlife.

- Great chance of seeing various whale species and breathtaking landscapes.

- Extras: A warm meal may be included depending on the tour package.

Tips for Choosing a Whale Watching Tour

- Check Reviews: Read reviews on platforms like TripAdvisor to gauge the experiences of previous participants.

- Tour Size: Consider whether you prefer a large boat with more amenities or a smaller group for a more intimate experience.

- Guarantees: Look for tours that offer guarantees on sightings, which can enhance your peace of mind.

- Additional Features: Consider any extra offerings, such as refreshments, educational content, or eco-friendly practices.

Marine Life to Look for on a Whale Watching Tour in Reykjavik

The waters surrounding Reykjavik, especially in **Faxaflói Bay,** are home to an impressive variety of marine life. While whales are the main attraction, you can also spot other fascinating sea creatures and birds. Here's an overview of the marine life you might encounter during your whale watching adventure:

1. Whales

- Humpback Whale:

- Characteristics: Large, acrobatic whales known for their spectacular breaching and tail-slapping.
    - Season: Most common from May to September.
    - Behavior: Frequently seen performing flips and tail displays, making them a highlight for photographers.

- Minke Whale:

- Characteristics: Sleek, small baleen whales, growing up to 10 meters in length.
    - Season: Visible year-round but more frequent in summer.
    - Behavior: Less dramatic than humpbacks, but their quick surfacing makes them exciting to watch.

- Orca (Killer Whale):

- Characteristics: Recognizable by their black and white coloring, orcas are apex predators.
   - Season: Can be seen year-round but are most commonly spotted in winter and spring.
   - Behavior: Often spotted in groups (pods), they are known for their hunting strategies and intelligence.

- Blue Whale:

- Characteristics: The largest animal on the planet, reaching up to 30 meters in length.
   - Season: Most frequently sighted in the summer.
   - Behavior: Due to their size, they are slower and more graceful in their movements, often displaying their massive backs while surfacing.

- Fin Whale:

- Characteristics: Second only to the blue whale in size, these whales are sleek and fast swimmers.
   - Season: Seen during the summer months.
   - Behavior: They often swim in pairs and are known for their speed and agility.

- Sei Whale:

- Characteristics: Rarely spotted, the sei whale is a medium-sized baleen whale, usually seen in deeper waters.
    - Season: Occasionally spotted in summer.

2. Dolphins and Porpoises

- White-Beaked Dolphin:

- Characteristics: Playful and social, these dolphins are common in Icelandic waters and are often seen alongside whale species.
    - Season: Year-round.
    - Behavior: Known for riding waves and jumping out of the water near boats.

- Harbour Porpoise:

- Characteristics: Smaller and more elusive than dolphins, porpoises are often shy but can be spotted near the surface.
    - Season: Year-round.
    - Behavior: Typically seen in small groups or alone, quickly surfacing before diving back into the water.

3. Seals

- Harbour Seal:

- Characteristics: Common along Iceland's coasts, these seals are curious and can often be seen lounging on rocks or swimming near the surface.
   - Season: Year-round.
   - Behavior: Often found in groups, they are playful and curious around boats.

- Grey Seal:

- Characteristics: Larger than the harbor seal, with a distinctive long nose, they are less common but still visible in some areas around Reykjavik.
   - Season: Year-round.
   - Behavior: They are often more solitary, but some colonies can be found on rocky shores.

4. Seabirds

- Atlantic Puffin:

- Characteristics: Iconic black and white seabirds with colorful beaks, puffins are a highlight during the summer months.
   - Season: Best seen from May to August, when they nest on cliffs and coastal islands.

- Behavior: Puffins are excellent divers and can be spotted near the water as they search for fish to feed their young.

- Northern Fulmar:

- Characteristics: Often confused with seagulls, fulmars are sturdy seabirds with a distinctive stiff-winged flight.
  - Season: Year-round.
  - Behavior: They are commonly seen flying near boats or riding the wind close to the waves.

- Gannets:

- Characteristics: Large seabirds known for their spectacular diving abilities. Gannets plunge into the sea from great heights to catch fish.
  - Season: Seen during summer.
  - Behavior: They can be seen hovering above before performing swift, impressive dives into the water.

- Arctic Tern:

- Characteristics: A migratory bird known for its long-distance travel; it flies from the Arctic to the Antarctic and back every year.
  - Season: Seen from May to July.
  - Behavior: They are agile fliers and can often be seen swooping above the water hunting for fish.

- Common Guillemot:

- Characteristics: A black and white seabird that nests in colonies along rocky cliffs.
  - Season: Summer.
  - Behavior: They dive into the sea for fish and can be spotted along the coast or flying in flocks.

5. Other Marine Life

- Jellyfish:
  - Lion's Mane Jellyfish: The largest jellyfish species, occasionally seen in Icelandic waters. Its trailing tentacles can reach up to 10 meters.
  - Moon Jellyfish: Common and smaller, these translucent jellyfish can sometimes be spotted near the surface of the water.

- Fish:

- Atlantic Cod: One of Iceland's most important fish species, commonly found in coastal waters.
  - Herring: Often spotted in schools, herring can attract large whales to feeding areas.
  - Capelin: A small fish that plays a vital role in the ecosystem as prey for many marine animals.

6. Other Wildlife

- Arctic Fox (On Land):

- Characteristics: While not marine life, the Arctic fox is Iceland's only native mammal. On land excursions near coastal areas, you might spot one.
   - Season: Year-round.

Geothermal Pools and Hot Springs Around Reykjavik

Iceland is famous for its geothermal activity, and Reykjavik is no exception. The capital and surrounding areas are home to a variety of geothermal pools and hot springs, where visitors can soak in naturally heated waters while enjoying stunning landscapes. These pools are an integral part of Icelandic culture and provide both relaxation and a connection to the earth's natural energy.

1. Blue Lagoon

- Location: 45 minutes from Reykjavik, near Keflavik International Airport.
   - Highlights: One of Iceland's most famous geothermal spas, the Blue Lagoon is renowned for its milky-blue waters rich in silica and minerals. The lagoon offers a luxurious bathing experience in a surreal volcanic

landscape.

- Features: Swim-up bar, in-water silica masks, sauna, steam rooms, and high-end spa treatments.

- Best for: Tourists looking for a premium geothermal experience, with wellness and relaxation amenities.

2. Sky Lagoon

- Location: 10-minute drive from Reykjavik city center.

- Highlights: A modern luxury lagoon with an infinity pool that merges with the Atlantic Ocean's horizon. The Sky Lagoon is inspired by Icelandic bathing traditions and offers breathtaking views of the North Atlantic and the city skyline.

- Features: Seven-step ritual that includes a cold plunge, sauna with ocean views, and a turf house-style bath.

- Best for: Those seeking a more intimate and scenic geothermal spa experience closer to the city.

3. Laugardalslaug

- Location: Reykjavik, in the Laugardalur Valley.

- Highlights: Reykjavik's largest public swimming pool, Laugardalslaug offers a combination of traditional pools and geothermal hot tubs. It's a local favorite and is ideal for those looking to experience a typical Icelandic public pool.

- Features: Multiple hot tubs, a steam bath, and an Olympic-size swimming pool.

- Best for: Budget-friendly geothermal experience, families, and those wanting to mix with locals.

4. Nauthólsvík Geothermal Beach

- Location: Reykjavik, south of the city center.

   - Highlights: This unique geothermal beach combines heated seawater with the cold North Atlantic. Nauthólsvík is a man-made beach with golden sand, where visitors can swim in both cold and hot water.

   - Features: Geothermal seawater lagoon, hot tubs, steam rooms.

   - Best for: Those looking for an outdoor hot spring experience with a mix of cold water swimming and beach activities.

5. Reykjadalur Hot Springs (Hot River)

- Location: 45-minute drive from Reykjavik, near Hveragerði.

   - Highlights: Reykjadalur, meaning "Steam Valley," offers a natural hot river where visitors can hike through a geothermal landscape to find secluded spots to bathe. This untouched, natural setting makes for a memorable experience.

   - Features: No developed facilities; a completely natural river heated by geothermal springs.

   - Best for: Adventurous travelers willing to hike to reach a more remote and natural hot spring.

6. Kleifarvatn Hot Springs

- Location: On the Reykjanes Peninsula, a 30-minute drive from Reykjavik.

   - Highlights: Kleifarvatn is a large lake surrounded by rugged volcanic scenery. While the lake itself is too cold for swimming, nearby geothermal springs offer hot spots for soaking. The area is known for its alien landscape with steam vents and boiling mud pools.

- Features: Natural hot springs, scenic volcanic terrain, and hiking opportunities.

- Best for: Nature lovers looking for a secluded, off-the-beaten-path geothermal experience.

7. Secret Lagoon

- Location: Near Flúðir, about a 90-minute drive from Reykjavik.

- Highlights: The Secret Lagoon is one of Iceland's oldest geothermal pools and offers a more rustic, less commercialized experience compared to the Blue Lagoon. Surrounded by natural hot springs and geysers, it provides a peaceful and scenic setting.

- Features: A naturally heated pool, small geysers, and walking paths around the geothermal area.

- Best for: Travelers seeking a more traditional and low-key geothermal experience.

8. Fontana Geothermal Baths

- Location: Laugarvatn, an hour's drive from Reykjavik.

- Highlights: Set on the shores of Lake Laugarvatn, Fontana is a relaxing geothermal spa offering hot pools and steam rooms heated by natural steam directly from the ground.

- Features: Multiple hot pools, natural steam baths, and the option to cool off with a swim in the cold lake.

- Best for: Those visiting the Golden Circle who want a more natural and serene bathing experience.

Benefits of Geothermal Pools

- Relaxation: The warm waters help soothe muscles and reduce stress.
 - Health: The minerals in geothermal water, like silica and sulfur, are believed to have therapeutic properties for the skin.
 - Cultural Experience: Bathing in geothermal pools is a deeply ingrained part of Icelandic culture, providing a way to connect with the country's traditions.

Tips for Enjoying Geothermal Pools

- Showering: It is customary (and often mandatory) to shower without a swimsuit before entering geothermal pools in Iceland.
 - Stay Hydrated: Soaking in hot water can be dehydrating, so remember to drink plenty of water.
 - Season: While the pools are enjoyable year-round, soaking in hot water during the winter months, surrounded by snow, can be especially magical.

Blue Lagoon

Overview

The Blue Lagoo is one of Iceland's most iconic and visited geothermal spas. Located in the middle of a dramatic lava field on the Reykjanes Peninsula, about a 45-minute drive from Reykjavik and 20 minutes from Keflavik International Airport, the Blue Lagoon is renowned for its striking milky-blue waters, rich in minerals like silica and sulfur, which are believed to have healing properties for the skin. The lagoon is a top destination for both tourists and locals alike, offering a luxurious and rejuvenating experience in a surreal volcanic setting.

Key Highlights

- Milky-Blue Waters: The geothermal seawater has a unique blue color due to the silica content that reflects light.
    - Health Benefits: The minerals, particularly silica and sulfur, are said to be beneficial for skin conditions, especially psoriasis, and for overall skin health.
    - Surreal Landscape: The lagoon is set against a backdrop of black lava fields and steaming vents, creating a tranquil and otherworldly atmosphere.

Features and Facilities

- Lagoon Pools: The expansive geothermal pool maintains a temperature of around 37–40°C (98–104°F) year-round, making it a perfect place to soak, even in winter.
    - Silica Mud Masks: Visitors are offered complimentary silica mud masks while bathing, believed to cleanse and exfoliate the skin.
    - In-Water Bars: The Blue Lagoon offers swim-up bars where you can enjoy a variety of beverages, including smoothies, beer, and wine, without leaving the comfort of the warm water.
    - Sauna and Steam Rooms: These are built into the lava rocks surrounding the lagoon, providing a relaxing way to warm up in between dips in the water.
    - Luxury Spa Treatments: The lagoon offers a wide range of spa

services, including in-water massages and various skin treatments, making it a wellness retreat for body and mind.

   - Restaurants: The LAVA Restaurant and Moss Restaurant provide fine dining options that feature Icelandic ingredients, with views overlooking the lagoon.

   - Blue Lagoon Retreat: A premium offering that includes access to a private lagoon, luxurious spa treatments, and upscale accommodations at the Retreat Hotel.

Best Time to Visit

- All Year Round: The Blue Lagoon is open year-round, and its waters remain warm even during the coldest months. Many visitors find it especially magical in winter, when they can bathe in the warm water while surrounded by snow.

   - Peak Season: June to August is the busiest time, so advance booking is essential during this period.

   - Northern Lights: Visiting during the winter months (October to March) also gives you a chance to experience the Northern Lights while soaking in the lagoon, a rare but stunning experience.

Ticket Options

- Comfort Package: Includes entrance to the Blue Lagoon, a silica mud mask, a towel, and one drink of your choice.

   - Premium Package: Includes everything in the Comfort package plus an additional algae mask, slippers, bathrobe, and a table reservation at the LAVA Restaurant with a glass of sparkling wine.

   - Retreat Spa: This exclusive package includes access to the private lagoon, luxurious spa treatments, and Retreat Hotel facilities.

Tips for Visiting

- Advance Booking: Due to its popularity, it's essential to book tickets in advance, especially during peak seasons. Same-day tickets are rarely available.
  - Shower Before Entering: As per Icelandic tradition, all visitors are required to shower naked before entering the lagoon to maintain cleanliness.
  - Protect Your Hair: The silica-rich water can dry out your hair, so it's a good idea to apply conditioner (provided in the showers) and tie long hair up before entering the water.
  - Avoid Jewelry: The minerals in the water can tarnish jewelry, so it's best to leave them in the lockers provided.
  - Stay Hydrated: While soaking in the warm water, it's easy to become dehydrated, so make sure to drink plenty of water, which is available around the lagoon.

How to Get There

- By Car: The Blue Lagoon is about 45 minutes by car from Reykjavik and 20 minutes from Keflavik International Airport. Many visitors stop here either on their way to or from the airport.
  - By Bus: There are regular bus services and shuttles from Reykjavik and Keflavik International Airport to the Blue Lagoon, making it easy to include in your travel itinerary.

Laugardalslaug

Overview

Laugardalslaug is the largest public swimming pool in Reykjavik and one of the most popular spots for both locals and tourists to experience Icelandic bathing culture. Located in the Laugardalur Valley, a short distance from Reykjavik's city center, this geothermal pool offers a more budget-friendly and authentic alternative to the luxury spas, providing a range of recreational facilities for all ages. It is a great place to unwind, meet locals, and experience daily life in Iceland.

Key Highlights

- Local Experience: Laugardalslaug is primarily frequented by Reykjavik residents, making it an ideal spot to experience the everyday Icelandic bathing tradition.
  - Geothermal Water: The pools are filled with naturally heated geothermal water, which is rich in minerals and maintains a comfortable temperature, perfect for relaxation.
  - Affordable Entry: Unlike luxury spas like the Blue Lagoon, Laugardalslaug offers a low-cost way to enjoy the benefits of geothermal bathing.

OUTDOOR ACTIVITIES IN REYKJAVIK

Features and Facilities

- Outdoor Geothermal Pool: The main attraction is the large outdoor swimming pool, which is heated to a comfortable 28°C (82°F). The pool is Olympic-sized, making it ideal for swimming laps.
  - Hot Tubs: There are several hot tubs of varying temperatures, ranging from 38°C to 44°C (100°F to 111°F), perfect for soaking and relaxing after a long day of sightseeing.
  - Children's Pool: The complex includes a shallow pool and water slides for children, making it a family-friendly destination.
  - Jacuzzi and Steam Room: Visitors can enjoy a jacuzzi and a steam bath, both popular for relaxation and rejuvenation.
  - Sauna: In addition to the outdoor pools, there is a traditional sauna available for those looking to sweat out toxins and enjoy some extra warmth.
  - Cold Plunge Pool: For the brave, there is a cold plunge pool that offers an invigorating contrast to the hot tubs, a practice believed to boost circulation.
  - Fitness Center and Sports Facilities: Laugardalslaug is located within the larger Laugardalur sports complex, which also includes a fitness center, football fields, and an athletics stadium.

Best Time to Visit

- Year-Round: Laugardalslaug is open all year, with the outdoor pools remaining warm even during the colder months. It is particularly pleasant in the winter, when you can relax in the hot tubs while surrounded by snow.
  - Weekdays: Visiting during the week is recommended if you prefer a quieter experience, as weekends can be busier with local families and

tourists.

Admission and Pricing

- Affordable Entry: Entrance fees are very reasonable, making it accessible for all travelers. Tickets cost around 900 ISK for adults and are lower for children, seniors, and those with Reykjavik City Cards.
  - Reykjavik City Card: If you have the Reykjavik City Card, entry to Laugardalslaug is free, making it a convenient option for those looking to explore the city's attractions on a budget.

What to Bring

- Swimsuit and Towel: You can bring your own swimsuit and towel, but both are available for rent if needed.
  - Shower Rules: Like all Icelandic pools, it is mandatory to shower without your swimsuit before entering the pool area. This is a strict hygiene rule in Iceland.

Getting There

- By Bus: Laugardalslaug is easily accessible by public transport from central Reykjavik. Several buses stop nearby, including lines 12 and 14.
  - By Car: If you have a rental car, there is ample parking available at the Laugardalur sports complex, where the pool is located.

Nearby Attractions

- Laugardalur Valley: Laugardalslaug is situated in the heart of Laugardalur Valley, an area that offers a range of other activities, including Reykjavik's botanical gardens, the Reykjavik Park and Zoo, and various walking paths.
  - Family-Friendly Activities: The nearby Family Park and Zoo is a great spot for families to visit before or after swimming, offering a chance to see Icelandic animals like reindeer and seals.

Secret Lagoon

Overview

The Secret Lagoon (Icelandic: Gamla Laugin) is one of Iceland's oldest and most beloved natural hot springs, offering a more intimate and authentic geothermal bathing experience compared to the more commercialized Blue Lagoon. Located in the small village of Flúðir in the Golden Circle region, about a 90-minute drive from Reykjavik, the Secret Lagoon is set in a picturesque landscape of bubbling geothermal springs, steaming vents, and moss-covered lava fields.

The lagoon's natural environment and laid-back atmosphere make it a perfect stop for those wanting to relax and soak in Iceland's geothermal waters in a peaceful, rustic setting.

Key Highlights

- Natural Hot Spring: The Secret Lagoon is fed by natural hot springs that maintain a temperature of around 38–40°C (100–104°F) year-round, offering a warm and soothing soak.
  - Historic Significance: Established in 1891, the Secret Lagoon is one of Iceland's oldest man-made pools, giving visitors a chance to experience a piece of Icelandic history while enjoying the hot springs.
  - Unspoiled Surroundings: The pool is surrounded by natural hot springs and small geysers that erupt every few minutes, adding to the scenic and tranquil atmosphere.
  - Less Crowded: Unlike the more famous Blue Lagoon, the Secret Lagoon offers a quieter and more serene experience, with fewer crowds and a more authentic, local vibe.

Features and Facilities

- Simple and Rustic: The Secret Lagoon has kept its traditional charm, with minimalistic facilities that enhance the natural beauty of the area. The pool itself is surrounded by rocks and geothermal features, giving it a rustic feel.
  - Hot Springs and Geysers: Visitors can watch small geysers erupt nearby and see natural hot springs bubbling around the pool, creating a unique geothermal landscape.
  - Changing Rooms and Showers: There are modern changing rooms with showers and lockers, where you can store your belongings and freshen up before entering the pool.
  - Snack Bar: A small on-site café offers snacks and beverages, including hot drinks for those visiting during colder months.

Best Time to Visit

- Year-Round: The Secret Lagoon is open year-round, and the water stays warm even in the coldest months. Winter visits can be particularly magical, as you can soak in the hot water while surrounded by snow or even catch a glimpse of the Northern Lights.
  - Morning or Late Afternoon: To avoid the peak hours of mid-day, it's best to visit in the morning or late afternoon, when the lagoon is less crowded.
  - Golden Circle Tours: Many visitors combine the Secret Lagoon with a Golden Circle tour, as it is located near popular attractions such as Gullfoss waterfall, Geysir, and Þingvellir National Park.

Ticket Options

- Standard Entry: Tickets are reasonably priced compared to other geothermal spas in Iceland. It is recommended to book your spot online in advance, as the Secret Lagoon has limited capacity.
  - Towel and Swimsuit Rental: If you don't bring your own, towels and swimsuits are available for rent on-site.

Tips for Visiting

- Bring a Swimsuit and Towel: While you can rent these items, it's recommended to bring your own to save on rental fees.
  - Shower Before Entering: As with all geothermal pools in Iceland, it's mandatory to shower without your swimsuit before entering the pool, following Icelandic hygiene rules.
  - Stay Hydrated: It's important to stay hydrated while soaking in hot

springs, so be sure to drink plenty of water before and after your visit.

   - Visit in Winter for Northern Lights: The lagoon is a fantastic place to visit in winter, especially at night, when you may get the chance to see the Northern Lights while soaking in the warm water.

How to Get There

- By Car: The Secret Lagoon is a 90-minute drive from Reykjavik and is easily accessible by car. Many visitors include it in a Golden Circle tour, as it is located near popular sites like Gullfoss and Geysir.

   - By Tour: There are numerous guided tours that include a visit to the Secret Lagoon as part of a day trip around the Golden Circle. These tours offer convenient transportation and guided commentary, making it a hassle-free way to experience the lagoon.

Nearby Attractions

- Golden Circle: The Secret Lagoon is a short drive from some of Iceland's most famous attractions, including Gullfoss, Geysir, and Þingvellir National Park. Many visitors combine a soak in the lagoon with a full day of exploring the Golden Circle.

   - Reykjadalur Valley: If you're looking for more hot spring experiences, the Reykjadalur Hot Spring River is another natural option for bathing, located within a short drive of the Secret Lagoon.

OUTDOOR ACTIVITIES IN REYKJAVIK

Exploring Nearby Nature

Reykjavik is surrounded by breathtaking natural landscapes, offering a wide range of outdoor activities and opportunities to explore Iceland's unique geological and environmental features. From volcanic craters and geothermal valleys to scenic coastlines and wildlife, the natural beauty around Reykjavik is easily accessible and perfect for adventurers, hikers, and nature lovers. Here are some of the must-visit natural areas near Reykjavik.

1. Þingvellir National Park

Distance from Reykjavik: 45 km (40-minute drive)
Key Highlights:
- UNESCO World Heritage Site: Þingvellir is one of Iceland's most historically and geologically significant sites. It's the birthplace of the world's first parliament, the Alþingi, and a natural wonder where the North American and Eurasian tectonic plates meet.
- Silfra Fissure: Famous for its crystal-clear water, this fissure allows you to snorkel or dive between two continents. It's one of the most unique diving spots in the world.
- Hiking: Numerous hiking trails wind through the park, offering views of waterfalls, cliffs, and volcanic landscapes.

2. Reykjadalur Hot Spring Valley

Distance from Reykjavik: 40 km (40-minute drive)
Key Highlights:
- Hot Spring River: The main attraction is a naturally warm river where visitors can bathe while surrounded by the stunning scenery of the geothermal valley.
- Hiking: The hike to the hot river is around 3 km (2 miles) and takes about an hour each way. The trail passes steaming vents, bubbling mud pools, and scenic valleys.
- Geothermal Activity: Reykjadalur is an excellent place to see Iceland's geothermal wonders in a less touristy and more remote setting.

3. Grótta Island Lighthouse

Distance from Reykjavik: 5 km (10-minute drive)
Key Highlights:
- Bird Watching: Grótta is a bird-watching haven, especially during the summer months when migratory birds such as Arctic terns nest in the area.
- Northern Lights Viewing: Due to its isolation and minimal light pollution, Grótta is one of the best spots near Reykjavik to see the Northern Lights in winter.
- Coastal Walks: The walk to Grótta takes you along Reykjavik's scenic coastline, with beautiful views of the Atlantic Ocean and distant mountains.

4. Heiðmörk Nature Reserve

Distance from Reykjavik: 15 km (20-minute drive)
　Key Highlights:
　- Lava Fields: Heiðmörk is home to expansive lava fields, dotted with wildflowers, trees, and unique rock formations. It's a peaceful retreat from the city, ideal for leisurely walks and picnics.
　- Rauðhólar: These striking red volcanic formations are located within the reserve and provide an incredible contrast to the surrounding greenery.
　- Hiking and Biking: The reserve offers a variety of trails for both hiking and cycling, ranging from easy to moderate difficulty, perfect for all ages.

5. Mount Esja

Distance from Reykjavik: 25 km (30-minute drive)
　Key Highlights:
　- Popular Hiking Destination: Mount Esja is one of Reykjavik's most popular hiking spots, offering multiple routes that vary in difficulty. The summit, Þverfellshorn, provides sweeping views of the city and the surrounding landscapes.
　- Accessible Trails: While some trails are suitable for beginners, others become steeper, offering a challenge for more experienced hikers.
　- Panoramic Views: On a clear day, the view from the summit includes Reykjavik, Faxaflói Bay, and the distant Reykjanes Peninsula.

6. Esjan Hiking Center

Located at the foot of Mount Esja, this hiking center offers facilities and information for those planning to hike the mountain. It's a great starting point for anyone new to the area.

7. Seltún Geothermal Area

Distance from Reykjavik: 40 km (45-minute drive)
  Key Highlights:
  - Vibrant Geothermal Landscape: Seltún features colorful mud pots, fumaroles, and hot springs. The area is known for its vibrant hues of red, yellow, and green due to the mineral deposits.
  - Easy Walking Trails: Wooden boardwalks lead visitors safely through the geothermal field, allowing them to observe the natural phenomena up close.
  - Photography Spot: The unique landscape, with its steam rising from the earth and brightly colored ground, makes Seltún a fantastic spot for photography.

8. Viðey Island

Distance from Reykjavik: Short ferry ride
  Key Highlights:
  - Historical Sites: Viðey Island has several historical sites, including the Viðey Church and Viðey House, which date back to the early 18th century.
  - Art Installations: The island is home to the Imagine Peace Tower, an art installation by Yoko Ono dedicated to John Lennon.

- Nature Walks: The island has peaceful walking trails and offers excellent views of Reykjavik's skyline from across the water.
- Birdlife: Like Grótta, Viðey is a great place for bird watching, with numerous species nesting on the island.

9. Snæfellsnes Peninsula

Distance from Reykjavik: 2-hour drive
Key Highlights:
- Snæfellsjökull Volcano: This glacier-covered volcano is a centerpiece of Snæfellsjökull National Park and is famous for being the setting of Jules Verne's novel Journey to the Center of the Earth.
- Kirkjufell Mountain: Known as "the most photographed mountain in Iceland," Kirkjufell and its surrounding waterfalls make for a breathtaking sight.
- Diverse Landscape: The peninsula is often called "Iceland in Miniature" because it contains so many of the country's natural features in one area, including volcanoes, lava fields, glaciers, waterfalls, and coastal cliffs.

10. Golden Circle

Distance from Reykjavik: 1-hour drive
Key Highlights:
- Gullfoss Waterfall: One of Iceland's most iconic waterfalls, Gullfoss features powerful cascading water in a canyon.
- Geysir Geothermal Area: Home to the famous Strokkur geyser, which erupts every 5–10 minutes, shooting boiling water high into the air.

- Þingvellir National Park: As previously mentioned, Þingvellir is part of the Golden Circle route and offers both historical significance and stunning natural beauty.

Þingvellir National Park

Location: 45 km northeast of Reykjavik
Travel Time: Approximately 40 minutes by car

Overview:

Þingvellir National Park, a UNESCO World Heritage Site, is one of Iceland's most significant historical and geological destinations. Not only is it home to the world's first democratic parliament, the Alþingi, established in 930 AD, but it's also where the North American and Eurasian tectonic plates meet, creating a dramatic rift valley.

Key Attractions:

1. Almannagjá Gorge:

This massive rift marks the divide between the North American and Eurasian tectonic plates. Visitors can walk through the gorge, which was also historically significant as the Alþingi assembly was held here. The path leads to panoramic views of Þingvellir and the surrounding area.

2. Silfra Fissure:

Silfra is one of the most famous diving and snorkeling sites in the world. Known for its incredibly clear water, which has over 100 meters of visibility, it allows adventurers to swim between two continents. The crystal-clear glacial water also provides a unique and tranquil underwater experience.

3. Öxarárfoss Waterfall:

This picturesque waterfall is located along the Almannagjá Gorge. It's a short hike from the visitor center and offers a great spot for photography. The waterfall was historically altered by humans to supply water to the Alþingi assembly, adding to its historical importance.

4. The Alþingi (Iceland's Parliament):

Þingvellir is the site where Iceland's parliament, Alþingi, was established in 930 AD, making it one of the oldest existing parliaments in the world. Although the original structures are no longer present, there are informational signs and markers highlighting its history.

5. Thingvallavatn Lake:

Iceland's largest natural lake, Thingvallavatn is an impressive sight within the park, offering stunning reflections of the surrounding mountains. The lake is home to a diverse ecosystem, including four species of Arctic char that have evolved separately over time. The surrounding landscape is ideal for photography and nature walks.

6. Hiking Trails:

Þingvellir offers numerous hiking trails that provide easy to moderate walks through stunning landscapes. Trails lead through volcanic fields, along rift valleys, and by pristine lakes. Visitors can explore on foot and enjoy the peace and natural beauty that the park has to offer.

7. Geological Wonders:

Þingvellir's unique geological location allows visitors to witness first-hand the ongoing separation of the tectonic plates, with the land visibly moving apart by about 2 cm each year. The dramatic cliffs and deep fissures create a spectacular landscape that tells the story of the Earth's constant transformation.

Outdoor Activities:

- Snorkeling and Diving:
    Silfra offers diving and snorkeling tours year-round, allowing visitors to explore the unique underwater environment between tectonic plates.

- Hiking:
    There are various well-marked trails suitable for all levels, whether you want a short walk or a full-day hike.

- Photography:
The park's natural beauty, including the lake, waterfalls, and volcanic scenery, provides endless opportunities for stunning photography.

Visitor Information:

- Opening Hours: Open year-round, 24 hours.
- Visitor Center: The Þingvellir Visitor Center provides historical exhibits, maps, and information about the park's significance.
- Entry Fee: While entrance to the park is free, there are parking fees.
- Best Time to Visit: Summer is ideal for hiking and exploring the natural beauty of the park. However, winter provides a magical atmosphere with snow and the chance to see the Northern Lights.

The Golden Circle

Overview:

The Golden Circle is Iceland's most popular tourist route, covering around 300 kilometers and offering a stunning mix of natural wonders, geological marvels, and historic sites. It encompasses three key attractions: Þingvellir National Park, the Geysir Geothermal Area, and Gullfoss Waterfall, all located within a relatively short distance from Reykjavik. The route is perfect for a day trip or can be explored over several days for a more relaxed experience.

Key Attractions:

1. Þingvellir National Park:

As covered previously, Þingvellir is both a geological and historical site. It's the starting point for many Golden Circle tours due to its proximity to Reykjavik and its deep cultural significance. Visitors can explore its dramatic rift valley, pristine lake, and learn about its ancient parliamentary history.

2. Geysir Geothermal Area:

Known for its active hot springs, the Geysir Geothermal Area is home to Iceland's most famous geyser, Strokkur, which erupts every 5-10 minutes, shooting boiling water up to 20-40 meters into the air. Though the original Great Geysir (which gave all geysers their name) is now dormant, the area remains highly geothermally active, with bubbling mud pools, steaming vents, and vibrant mineral deposits.

- Strokkur Geyser: The star of the show, Strokkur reliably erupts throughout the day, making it a must-see spectacle for visitors.
  - Geothermal Hot Springs: In addition to geysers, the area is dotted with small hot springs, fumaroles, and mineral-rich water pools, creating a visually striking geothermal landscape.

Travel Tip: Be sure to stay a safe distance from the hot springs and geysers as the water is extremely hot and the eruptions can be sudden.

3. Gullfoss Waterfall:

Often referred to as the "Golden Waterfall," Gullfoss is one of Iceland's most iconic and powerful waterfalls. The Hvítá River cascades in two dramatic stages into a deep canyon, creating a spectacular display of nature's power. On sunny days, visitors are treated to rainbows forming over the mist, enhancing the already breathtaking scene.

- Viewpoints: There are several viewing platforms along the trail leading up to the waterfall, offering various perspectives of the falls and the surrounding canyon.
  - Hiking: The walking paths provide easy access to different viewpoints, allowing visitors to get up close to the roaring falls or view it from a higher vantage point.
  - Winter Visit: In winter, the frozen landscape adds a magical quality to Gullfoss, with the falls surrounded by snow and ice. However, visitors should take caution on the sometimes slippery paths.

4. Kerið Crater Lake (Optional Stop):

Located slightly off the main Golden Circle route, Kerið is a striking volcanic crater filled with vivid blue water. The red volcanic rock contrasts beautifully with the water, making it a visually unique and lesser-known stop. Visitors can walk around the rim or descend into the crater to explore the lake up close.

- Hiking: The crater's circular rim offers an easy hike with excellent views over the lake and the surrounding area.
  - Geological Significance: Kerið is estimated to be about 3,000 years old and is one of several volcanic craters in the area, but its unusually

shallow bowl-like shape makes it stand out.

Outdoor Activities:

- Hiking:
There are numerous trails around the Golden Circle, ranging from easy walks around the attractions to more strenuous hikes in the surrounding landscape.

- Geothermal Experiences:
Some tours offer stops at smaller, less crowded geothermal hot springs where you can relax in naturally heated waters, adding a soothing break to your adventure.

- Snowmobiling & Super Jeep Tours:
For the more adventurous, some tour operators offer snowmobiling on nearby glaciers or super jeep tours, which allow you to explore more remote areas and access off-the-beaten-path attractions along the Golden Circle.

- Photography:
The Golden Circle offers incredible photo opportunities year-round, from the colorful geothermal areas to the powerful waterfalls and unique volcanic landscapes.

Self-Guided vs. Guided Tours:

- Self-Guided Tours:
Many visitors choose to rent a car and explore the Golden Circle at their own pace. Roads are well-maintained and easy to navigate. With a self-guided tour, you have the freedom to choose how long to stay at each site and can discover hidden gems along the way.

- Guided Tours:
There are numerous guided tours available, ranging from half-day trips to full-day excursions. Tours often include additional stops or activities, such as visits to local farms, snowmobiling on Langjökull Glacier, or soaking in geothermal pools.

Best Time to Visit:

- Summer (June to August):
The long daylight hours and warmer temperatures make summer the most popular time to visit. The landscape is lush and green, and all attractions are easily accessible.

-Winter (November to March):
Winter offers the chance to see the Northern Lights and explore a snow-covered landscape. Roads are generally well-maintained, but visitors should be prepared for icy conditions. Gullfoss and the Geysir area look particularly stunning with a dusting of snow, and fewer tourists make for a more tranquil experience.

Practical Tips:

- Clothing:
The weather can change rapidly, so it's important to wear layers and waterproof clothing. Even in summer, the weather can be cool and windy, especially around Gullfoss.

- Driving:
If driving the Golden Circle, be cautious of winter road conditions and always check the weather forecast and road safety updates before setting out.

Snæfellsnes Peninsula

Overview:

The Snæfellsnes Peninsula is often referred to as "Iceland in Miniature" due to its diverse landscapes that encompass volcanoes, glaciers, waterfalls, lava fields, charming fishing villages, and dramatic coastlines. Located approximately 120 kilometers northwest of Reykjavik, the peninsula offers a wealth of outdoor activities and stunning natural beauty, making it a popular destination for day trips and extended visits.

Key Attractions:

1. Snæfellsjökull National Park:

Dominated by the iconic Snæfellsjökull Glacier, this national park is a UNESCO Global Geopark known for its stunning landscapes and geological features. The glacier-capped stratovolcano stands at 1,446 meters and is the centerpiece of the park.

- Snæfellsjökull Glacier:
    Adventurers can hike or take guided glacier tours on Snæfellsjökull, enjoying breathtaking views of the surrounding landscape from the summit. The glacier is also said to be a mystical site, inspiring various literary works, including Jules Verne's Journey to the Center of the Earth.

- Djúpalónssandur Beach:
    A black pebble beach surrounded by steep cliffs, Djúpalónssandur features unique rock formations and remnants of a shipwreck. The beach is a great place for a scenic walk and offers stunning views of Snæfellsjökull.

- Saxhóll Crater:
    This volcanic crater is a short hike from the parking area and provides panoramic views of the national park and surrounding coastline.

2. Kirkjufell Mountain and Kirkjufellsfoss Waterfall:

One of Iceland's most photographed landmarks, Kirkjufell (463 meters) is a picturesque mountain often featured in travel brochures. The adjacent Kirkjufellsfoss waterfall creates a perfect foreground for stunning photographs, particularly during sunrise or sunset.

- Hiking:
   Several hiking trails in the area provide opportunities to explore the landscape and capture the beauty of Kirkjufell from different angles.

3. Arnarstapi and Hellnar:

These two charming coastal villages are connected by a scenic walking path along the cliffs, featuring stunning views of sea stacks and unique rock formations.

- Arnarstapi:
   Known for its picturesque harbor and basalt columns, the village offers several hiking options and is home to the striking Gatklettur arch rock.

- Hellnar:
   A small fishing village with a quaint café and restaurant, Hellnar is the perfect spot to rest after exploring the coastline.

4. Búðakirkja (Black Church of Búðir):

This iconic black church is located near the Búðahraun lava field and surrounded by a stunning landscape, including mountains and a coastal view. It's a popular photography spot and a serene place for reflection.

5. Lóndrangar Basalt Cliffs:

The Lóndrangar sea stacks rise majestically from the sea, remnants of a volcanic crater. The cliffs are home to various seabirds, making it a great spot for birdwatching, especially during the summer months.

6. Rauðfeldsgjá Gorge:

A stunning gorge with steep cliffs, Rauðfeldsgjá offers a short hike into the depths of the mountain. Visitors can explore the gorge and enjoy the beautiful waterfalls cascading down its sides.

Outdoor Activities:

- Hiking:
  Snæfellsnes is home to numerous hiking trails, catering to all skill levels. Trails vary from short walks along the coast to more challenging hikes in the national park and up to Snæfellsjökull Glacier.

- Birdwatching:
  The peninsula is a haven for birdwatchers, with numerous species nesting along the cliffs and shores, especially in the summer months.

- Whale Watching:
  Tours from nearby towns like Ólafsvík offer whale watching opportunities. Common species include orcas, humpback whales, and minke whales.

- Fishing:
The waters around Snæfellsnes are known for excellent fishing, with options for both freshwater and saltwater fishing available.

- Caving:
Explore the unique lava caves, such as Vatnshellir Cave, located within Snæfellsjökull National Park. Guided tours provide insights into the geological history and formation of these caves.

Best Time to Visit:

- Summer (June to August):
With long daylight hours and mild weather, summer is ideal for outdoor activities, including hiking, birdwatching, and exploring the coast.

- Winter (November to March):
Winter offers a chance to see the Northern Lights and experience the beautiful snowy landscapes, but visitors should be prepared for cold weather and possible road closures.

Getting There:

- By Car:
The Snæfellsnes Peninsula is easily accessible by car, with well-maintained roads leading from Reykjavik. The drive offers stunning scenery along the way.

- Tours:

Many tour operators offer day trips to Snæfellsnes from Reykjavik, often including guided hikes and sightseeing.

Practical Tips:

- Clothing:

Dress in layers and be prepared for rapidly changing weather conditions. Waterproof clothing and sturdy hiking boots are recommended.

- Road Conditions:

Check weather and road conditions before traveling, especially in winter when conditions can change quickly.

Day Trips from Reykjavik

South Coast Adventures

The South Coast of Iceland is renowned for its breathtaking landscapes, dramatic waterfalls, black sand beaches, and glacial vistas. Stretching from Reykjavik to Vík í Mýrdal, this region offers an array of outdoor activities and must-visit sights that showcase the natural beauty of Iceland. Below is a comprehensive guide to the top attractions and adventures along the South Coast.

Key Attractions:

1. Seljalandsfoss Waterfall:

One of Iceland's most iconic waterfalls, Seljalandsfoss drops 60 meters (197 feet) over a cliff, allowing visitors to walk behind it for a unique perspective.

- Adventure:

The short path leading behind the waterfall offers an exhilarating experience, especially on sunny days when rainbows can form in the mist.

2. Skógafoss Waterfall:

Another stunning waterfall, Skógafoss stands at 60 meters tall and is one of the largest in the country. A staircase beside the waterfall allows visitors to hike to the top for panoramic views of the surrounding landscape.

- Adventure:
 The area offers several hiking trails, including the popular Fimmvörðuháls trek, which leads toward the glaciers and offers stunning scenery.

3. Sólheimasandur Plane Wreck:

The haunting remains of a U.S. Navy DC-3 plane lie on the black sands of Sólheimasandur beach. The wreck is accessible via a 4 km (2.5 miles) walk from the parking area.

- Adventure:
 A visit to the wreck is a popular photography spot, especially at sunrise or sunset, providing a unique juxtaposition against the stark landscape.

4. Reynisfjara Black Sand Beach:

Famous for its black pebbles, basalt columns, and powerful waves, Reynisfjara beach near the town of Vík is a must-visit. The dramatic sea stacks, Reynisdrangar, rise from the ocean, adding to the surreal beauty.

- Adventure:
   Explore the beach and its unique rock formations, but be cautious of the strong waves and sneaker waves, which can be dangerous.

5. Dyrhólaey Arch:

This natural rock arch offers stunning views of the surrounding cliffs and coastline. The area is also a prime spot for birdwatching, particularly puffins during the summer months.

- Adventure:
   Hike to the top of the arch for breathtaking views of the black sand beach and the sea stacks.

6. Mýrdalsjökull Glacier:

The fourth-largest glacier in Iceland, Mýrdalsjökull is located above the village of Vík and offers various outdoor activities.

- Adventure:
   Guided glacier hikes and ice climbing tours are popular, allowing visitors to explore the glacier's crevasses and ice formations safely.

7. Vatnajökull National Park:

This vast national park is home to Europe's largest glacier, Vatnajökull, and features stunning glacial landscapes, waterfalls, and hiking trails.

- Adventure:

Join a guided glacier walk or take a snowmobile tour for an exhilarating experience on the glacier's surface.

Outdoor Activities:

1. Hiking:

The South Coast offers a variety of hiking opportunities, from short walks to challenging multi-day treks. Notable trails include:

- Fimmvörðuháls:
    A challenging hike between Skógafoss and Þórsmörk, offering stunning views of waterfalls, glaciers, and volcanic landscapes.

- Skaftafell National Park:
    With trails leading to waterfalls, glaciers, and panoramic viewpoints, this park is a hiker's paradise.

2. Ice Climbing:

Ice climbing tours are available on Mýrdalsjökull and Vatnajökull glaciers, offering a thrilling way to experience Iceland's icy landscapes.

3. Glacier Hiking:

Join a guided glacier hike to explore crevasses, ice caves, and the breathtaking scenery of the glaciers.

4. Whale Watching:

While not as common on the South Coast as in other areas, some tours operate from nearby towns, offering opportunities to see various marine life.

5. Horseback Riding:

Explore the scenic landscapes on horseback, experiencing Icelandic horses' unique gait and friendly nature.

6. Photography:

The diverse landscapes of the South Coast provide countless opportunities for stunning photography, especially during sunrise and sunset.

Best Time to Visit:

- Summer (June to August):
Ideal for hiking, birdwatching, and enjoying the midnight sun. Temperatures are mild, and access to trails and attractions is at its peak.

- Winter (December to February):
Offers a chance to see the Northern Lights and explore snow-covered landscapes. Be prepared for cold weather and possible road closures.

Getting There:

- By Car:
Renting a car is the best way to explore the South Coast, allowing flexibility to stop at various attractions along the route. The drive from Reykjavik takes about 2 to 3 hours.

- Tours:
Many operators offer guided day tours from Reykjavik, providing transportation and guided experiences at key attractions.

Practical Tips:

- Clothing:
Dress in layers and prepare for rapidly changing weather conditions.

Waterproof clothing and sturdy footwear are essential for outdoor activities.

- Road Conditions:
Check weather and road conditions before traveling, especially during winter when conditions can change quickly.

- Safety:
Always respect safety guidelines when visiting natural attractions, particularly near waterfalls and beaches.

Seljalandsfoss and Skógafoss Waterfalls

The South Coast of Iceland is home to some of the country's most iconic waterfalls, including Seljalandsfoss and Skógafoss. Both of these natural wonders offer breathtaking views and unique experiences, making them must-visit destinations for travelers. Here's a closer look at each waterfall, including what to expect and activities to enjoy.

Seljalandsfoss Waterfall

Overview:

Seljalandsfoss is one of Iceland's most famous and photographed waterfalls, known for its striking beauty and unique feature of allowing visitors to walk behind the cascading water. It drops approximately 60 meters (197 feet) from the cliffs of the former coastline, creating a stunning spectacle.

Access:

- Location: Located along Route 1 (the Ring Road), about 30 km (18 miles) west of Vík and 120 km (75 miles) southeast of Reykjavik.
  - Parking: There is a parking area close to the waterfall with a small fee.

What to Expect:

- Walk Behind the Falls: A well-marked path allows you to walk behind the waterfall for a unique perspective. Be prepared to get wet from the mist, especially on windy days.
  - Photography: The waterfall is especially beautiful at sunset, and rainbows often form in the spray on sunny days, making for stunning photographs.
  - Surrounding Area: There are walking paths around the waterfall that provide different vantage points and views of the surrounding landscape.

Activities:

- Hiking: The trail leading up to the waterfall connects to the longer Fimmvörðuháls trek, which continues toward Þórsmörk and offers breathtaking views.
  - Nature Walks: Explore the surrounding area, which features lush greenery and unique rock formations.

Skógafoss Waterfall

Overview:

Skógafoss is another of Iceland's majestic waterfalls, standing at 60 meters (197 feet) high and 25 meters (82 feet) wide. It is one of the largest waterfalls in the country and is known for its powerful flow and stunning rainbows that often appear on sunny days.

Access:
  - Location: Situated along the Ring Road, about 30 km (18 miles) northwest of Vík and 150 km (93 miles) southeast of Reykjavik.
  - Parking: A parking lot is available near the waterfall, and there is no fee for parking.

What to Expect:

- Staircase to the Top: A staircase with 527 steps leads to an observation platform above the waterfall, providing a panoramic view of the falls and the surrounding landscape.
  - Powerful Flow: Skógafoss has a strong flow, which creates a mist that can lead to rainbows in sunny conditions, making it a popular spot for photographers.
  - Surrounding Area: The area around Skógafoss is picturesque, with lush green hills and the Skógá River flowing into the Atlantic Ocean.

Activities:
  - Hiking: The Fimmvörðuháls trail starts here, leading hikers through a dramatic landscape filled with waterfalls, volcanic craters, and valleys.

- Exploring Skógar: Visit the nearby Skógar Museum, which showcases Icelandic history, culture, and traditional turf houses.

Practical Tips for Visiting Seljalandsfoss and Skógafoss

- Best Time to Visit: Both waterfalls can be visited year-round, but summer (June to August) offers the best weather for hiking and exploring. Spring (April to May) also brings beautiful blooms and lush greenery.

- Safety Precautions: Always be cautious near the waterfalls, especially on wet rocks and paths. The spray can create slippery surfaces. When walking behind Seljalandsfoss, be aware of changing weather conditions.

- Photography: Early morning or late afternoon is the best time for photography, as the sunlight casts beautiful light on the falls. Bring waterproof gear for your camera if you plan to walk behind Seljalandsfoss.

- Visitor Amenities: There are restroom facilities available at both waterfalls, but food options may be limited, so it's a good idea to bring snacks and water.

Reynisfjara Black Sand Beach

Overview:
  Reynisfjara is one of the most famous black sand beaches in Iceland, located near the village of Vík í Mýrdal on the southern coast. Renowned for its dramatic landscape, stunning basalt columns, and powerful Atlantic waves, Reynisfjara offers a unique and breathtaking experience for visitors. It's a popular spot for photographers, nature lovers, and those looking to explore the raw beauty of Iceland's coastline.

Access

- Location: Reynisfjara is situated about 12 km (7.5 miles) east of Vík, along the Ring Road (Route 1).
  - Parking: There is a designated parking lot near the beach, with no fee for parking. Be sure to follow local parking regulations.

What to Expect

- Black Sand: The beach's unique black sand is composed of volcanic basalt, giving it a striking appearance against the backdrop of the white waves crashing onto the shore.
  - Basalt Columns: One of the standout features of Reynisfjara is the stunning basalt column formations. These natural structures, created by volcanic activity, resemble giant stepping stones and provide a dramatic setting for photography.

- Reynisdrangar Sea Stacks: Just offshore, you'll see the iconic Reynisdrangar sea stacks, towering basalt formations that rise dramatically from the ocean. According to folklore, these stacks are trolls turned to stone by the sunlight.

- Cave Exploration: At the western end of the beach, you can find a large basalt cave known as Hálsanefshellir. This cave showcases beautiful geological formations and is a great spot for exploration.

Activities

- Photography: Reynisfjara is a photographer's paradise. The contrast of the black sand with the white surf and the colorful cliffs creates stunning visuals. Sunrise and sunset offer particularly beautiful lighting for photos.

- Beach Walks: Enjoy a leisurely walk along the beach, taking in the breathtaking views of the sea stacks, cliffs, and surrounding landscapes. Be mindful of the strong waves and sneaker waves that can be dangerous.

- Birdwatching: The cliffs near Reynisfjara are home to numerous seabirds, including puffins during the summer months. Bring binoculars for a closer look at these fascinating birds.

Safety Precautions

- Strong Waves: Reynisfjara is known for its dangerous rip currents and sudden waves, known as "sneaker waves." Always keep a safe distance from the water's edge and heed any warning signs.

- Weather Conditions: The weather can change rapidly in Iceland. Dress in layers and be prepared for wind and rain, even during summer.
  - Respect Nature: Stay on marked paths and respect the natural environment. The beach is a delicate ecosystem, and it's important to leave no trace.

Nearby Attractions

- Vík í Mýrdal: The charming village of Vík is just a short drive away. Visit the local church, enjoy a meal at a café, or explore the local shops.
  - Dyrhólaey: This nearby promontory offers stunning views of Reynisfjara, the sea stacks, and the surrounding coastline. It's also a great spot for birdwatching, particularly for puffins in the summer months.
  - Skógafoss and Seljalandsfoss: These iconic waterfalls are located along the South Coast and can easily be combined with a visit to Reynisfjara for a full day of exploration.

Glacier Hiking at Sólheimajökull

Overview:

Sólheimajökull is one of Iceland's most accessible glaciers, located on the southern coast near Vík í Mýrdal. As a part of the larger Mýrdalsjökull glacier, Sólheimajökull offers stunning ice formations, crevasses, and breathtaking views, making it a popular destination for glacier hiking. Whether you are a seasoned hiker or a beginner, a glacier hike here provides a unique opportunity to explore Iceland's incredible glacial landscapes.

Access

- Location: Sólheimajökull is situated approximately 30 km (18.6 miles) northwest of Vík, along Route 1 (the Ring Road).
  - Parking: There is a designated parking area near the glacier's edge. Be sure to follow any posted guidelines and park only in designated areas.

What to Expect

- Glacier Terrain: Expect to traverse a variety of terrain, including ice formations, deep crevasses, and stunning blue ice caves. The glacier's surface can vary, so prepare for an adventurous trek.
  - Spectacular Views: The hike offers panoramic views of the surrounding landscape, including mountains, valleys, and the ocean in the distance. The contrast of the white glacier against the black volcanic soil is particularly striking.
  - Ice Features: You'll see various ice features such as seracs (tall towers of ice), crevasses, and meltwater pools, which change with the seasons.

Guided Tours

Safety Note: It is highly recommended to join a guided tour for glacier hiking. Experienced guides are familiar with the glacier's conditions and can ensure your safety while providing valuable information about the glacier's geology and environment.

- Tour Options: Various companies offer guided glacier hikes, which may include:
    - Half-Day Hikes: These typically last 2-4 hours and are perfect for beginners or those short on time.
    - Full-Day Hikes: Longer excursions may include more challenging routes and additional exploration.
    - Combo Tours: Some tours combine glacier hiking with other activities, such as ice climbing or visits to nearby waterfalls and attractions.

What to Bring on the Tour:
    - Clothing: Wear warm, layered clothing that can handle cold and windy conditions. Waterproof and windproof outer layers are essential.
    - Footwear: Sturdy, waterproof hiking boots are required. Most tours provide crampons (spiked traction devices) to attach to your boots for added grip on the ice.
    - Safety Gear: Guides will provide essential gear, including harnesses, ropes, and helmets, as needed.

Tips for Glacier Hiking

- Physical Fitness: Glacier hiking requires a moderate level of fitness, so be prepared for some physical exertion. The hikes can be challenging but are generally suitable for most individuals.
  - Stay with Your Group: Always stay with your group and follow the guide's instructions to ensure everyone's safety.
  - Respect the Environment: Glaciers are sensitive ecosystems. Stay on marked paths and avoid stepping on delicate ice formations or areas that are not designated for hiking.

Nearby Attractions

- Sólheimasandur Plane Wreck: A short hike from the parking area leads to the famous US Navy DC-3 plane wreck, which crashed on the black sand beach in 1973.
  - Reynisfjara Black Sand Beach: Just a short drive from Sólheimajökull, Reynisfjara offers stunning views and unique geological features, including basalt columns and sea stacks.
  - Skógafoss and Seljalandsfoss: These iconic waterfalls are easily accessible from Sólheimajökull and make for great photo opportunities and exploration.

Snorkeling and Diving in Iceland

Overview:
Iceland offers some of the most unique snorkeling and diving experiences in the world, primarily due to its stunning underwater landscapes, crystal-clear waters, and geothermal features. The most famous location for these activities is Silfra Fissure, located in Þingvellir National Park, where divers can literally swim between the North American and Eurasian tectonic plates. Whether you're a beginner or an experienced diver, snorkeling and diving in Iceland provide an unforgettable adventure.

Best Locations for Snorkeling and Diving

1. Silfra Fissure

- Description: Silfra is a rift between the North American and Eurasian tectonic plates. Its waters are renowned for their clarity, visibility often exceeding 100 meters (328 feet), thanks to glacial meltwater filtering through lava fields for decades.
 - Activities:
 - Snorkeling: Snorkelers can float along the fissure, enjoying the stunning underwater scenery, including unique rock formations and vibrant algae.
 - Diving: Divers can explore the deep, cold waters and experience the thrill of being in one of the world's most geologically significant sites.
 - Guided Tours: Most snorkeling and diving at Silfra is done through guided tours, which include all necessary gear and safety equipment.

2. Lake Thingvallavatn

- Description: Located within Þingvellir National Park, this lake offers excellent diving conditions, especially for more experienced divers.
  - Activities:
  - Diving: Explore submerged volcanic landscapes and various fish species. The visibility is good, but diving here requires a certain level of certification and experience.
  - Tours: Guided tours often include transportation and equipment rental.

3. Skaftafell National Park

- Description: This area is known for its incredible glaciers and dramatic landscapes. Certain spots in the park offer diving opportunities in glacial lakes.
  - Activities:
  - Diving: Experience the cold waters and stunning ice formations. This is typically for more advanced divers, as conditions can be challenging.
  - Guided Tours: Check local dive shops for guided tours in the area.

4. Reykjavik

- Description: Some dive shops in Reykjavik offer excursions to nearby snorkeling and diving spots, including the Atlantic Ocean.
  - Activities:
  - Diving: Explore marine life, including colorful fish and unique rock formations. Visibility varies, so check conditions ahead of time.

- Day Trips: Many dive shops offer day trips to popular spots for both snorkeling and diving.

What to Expect

- Water Temperature: The water temperature in Icelandic waters can be quite cold, ranging from 2°C to 4°C (36°F to 39°F), particularly in Silfra. Participants will typically wear drysuits or wetsuits, depending on the location and season.
- Marine Life: While not as diverse as tropical locations, you may encounter various fish species, including Arctic char and perch, along with fascinating geological features underwater.
- Stunning Scenery: The combination of unique underwater landscapes, clear blue waters, and the experience of swimming between tectonic plates creates an unforgettable visual experience.

Safety Precautions

- Guided Tours: Always participate in guided snorkeling or diving tours, especially if you are inexperienced. Professional guides will provide safety briefings, equipment, and ensure you are familiar with the conditions.
- Physical Fitness: Ensure you are in good physical condition. Snorkeling and diving can be physically demanding, and participants should be comfortable in cold water.
- Check Equipment: If renting gear, check that it fits properly and is in good condition. Drysuits should be inspected for leaks.

- Weather Conditions: Be aware that Icelandic weather can change rapidly. Dress in layers and be prepared for wind and rain, even in summer.

Tips for Snorkeling and Diving

- Book in Advance: Popular tours can fill up quickly, especially during the peak season (June to August). It's best to book ahead.
  - Dress Appropriately: Even though you'll be in a wetsuit or drysuit, it's a good idea to wear thermal layers underneath and bring warm clothing for before and after your experience.
  - Stay Hydrated: Drinking water is essential, especially if you're participating in multiple activities during the day.

Silfra Fissure

Overview:

Silfra Fissure, located in Þingvellir National Park, is one of Iceland's most famous natural wonders and a prime destination for snorkeling and diving. It is the only place in the world where you can snorkel or dive between two tectonic plates—North America and Eurasia. The fissure is filled with glacial meltwater that has been filtered through volcanic rock, resulting in incredibly clear water with visibility often exceeding 100 meters (328 feet).

Geography and Geology

- Formation: Silfra is a rift formed by the divergence of the North American and Eurasian tectonic plates. As these plates pull apart, the fissure continues to grow, creating a unique underwater landscape.
    - Depth: The fissure ranges from 10 to 63 meters (33 to 207 feet) deep, providing various depths for both snorkeling and diving enthusiasts.
    - Water Source: The water in Silfra comes from the Langjökull glacier, which melts and flows into the fissure. This water is extremely clean and clear, thanks to its long filtration process through volcanic rock.

Snorkeling and Diving Experience

- Snorkeling:
    - What to Expect: Snorkelers float on the surface, marveling at the vibrant blue water, unique underwater rock formations, and lush green algae. The experience is surreal, as the clarity allows you to see deep into the fissure.
    - Equipment: Snorkeling tours typically provide drysuits to keep you warm in the cold water, along with all necessary gear, including masks, snorkels, and fins.
    - Guided Tours: It is essential to book a guided tour to ensure safety and gain insight into the geology and ecology of the area.

- Diving:
    - What to Expect: Divers can explore the deeper parts of the fissure, navigating through crevasses and unique geological formations. The underwater scenery includes dramatic rock walls and stunning ice

formations.
  - Certification Requirements: Divers must have an Open Water Certification or equivalent, as conditions can be challenging. Some tours may offer advanced dives for experienced divers.
  - Safety Gear: All necessary diving equipment, including tanks, weights, and wetsuits or drysuits, is provided by the tour operators.

Best Time to Visit

- Season: Silfra is open year-round for snorkeling and diving, although the peak season is from June to September. During these months, the weather is milder, and the water temperature can be slightly warmer (around 2-4°C or 36-39°F).
  - Winter Visits: Diving and snorkeling in winter can be magical, as the snow-covered landscape adds to the beauty of the experience. However, proper cold-water gear is essential.

What to Bring

- Warm Clothing: Dress in layers before putting on your drysuit. It's crucial to stay warm while preparing for your dive or snorkel.
  - Waterproof Gear: Bring a waterproof bag for your belongings, as you'll be near water.
  - Camera: If you're interested in underwater photography, consider bringing an underwater camera or a GoPro, but check with your tour operator about their policies on equipment.

Environmental Considerations

- Leave No Trace: Visitors must respect the natural environment by following guidelines set by tour operators. Do not disturb the fragile ecosystem.
  - Stay on Marked Paths: When exploring the area around Silfra, stick to designated trails to protect the local flora and fauna.

Nearby Attractions

- Þingvellir National Park: This UNESCO World Heritage site is home to stunning landscapes, historic significance, and other geological features, including lava fields and waterfalls.
  - Öxarárfoss Waterfall: A beautiful waterfall located within Þingvellir National Park, easily accessible and a great spot for photos.
  - Drekkingarhylur (Drowning Pool): An area of historical significance located in the park, where convicted criminals were executed in the past.

Here are some of the best tours for snorkeling at Silfra Fissure in Iceland, providing different experiences and options based on your preferences:

1. Silfra Snorkeling Tour by Dive.is

- Overview: Dive.is is one of the most reputable dive and snorkeling operators in Iceland, offering guided tours specifically focused on Silfra.
  - Inclusions:
  - Professional guide
  - All snorkeling gear (drysuits, fins, masks, snorkels)
  - Transport from Reykjavik to Þingvellir National Park
  - Complimentary hot chocolate and snacks
  - Duration: Approximately 3-4 hours, with about 30-40 minutes of snorkeling.
  - Website: [Dive.is](https://www.dive.is)

2. Snorkeling in Silfra by Arctic Adventures

- Overview: Arctic Adventures provides a variety of outdoor tours, including snorkeling in Silfra, focusing on safety and customer experience.
  - Inclusions:
  - Professional snorkeling guide
  - Drysuit and all snorkeling gear
  - Transportation from Reykjavik
  - Photos of your experience (available for purchase)
  - Duration: Approximately 3-4 hours, including snorkeling time.
  - Website: [Arctic Adventures](https://www.adventures.is)

3. Silfra Snorkeling Tour by Viking Breathe

- Overview: Viking Breathe offers small-group snorkeling tours in Silfra, emphasizing a personalized experience.
  - Inclusions:
  - Small group sizes (max 6 people)
  - All snorkeling equipment (drysuit, fins, etc.)
  - Transport from Reykjavik
  - Hot drinks and snacks
  - Duration: Around 3-4 hours, including the snorkeling session.
  - Website: [Viking Breathe](https://www.vikingbreathe.is)

4. Silfra Snorkeling Adventure by Snorkeling Iceland

- Overview: Snorkeling Iceland specializes in snorkeling tours, providing detailed information about the area's geology and ecology.
  - Inclusions:
  - Experienced guides
  - All necessary snorkeling gear
  - Transport from Reykjavik
  - Snacks and hot drinks
  - Duration: Approximately 3-4 hours, with time for underwater exploration.
  - Website: [Snorkeling Iceland](https://snorkelingiceland.com)

5. Silfra Snorkeling Combo Tour by Reykjavik Excursions

- Overview: This tour combines snorkeling in Silfra with other popular attractions in the Þingvellir National Park area.
    - Inclusions:
    - Guided snorkeling in Silfra
    - Visit to nearby attractions, including Öxarárfoss
    - All necessary gear and transport from Reykjavik
    - Duration: Approximately 6-8 hours, depending on the additional sites visited.
    - Website: [Reykjavik Excursions](https://www.reykjavikexcursions.is)

6. Ultimate Silfra Snorkeling Tour by Extreme Iceland

- Overview: This tour is aimed at those seeking an adventurous experience, combining snorkeling with a more in-depth exploration of Þingvellir National Park.
    - Inclusions:
    - All snorkeling gear and drysuits
    - Professional guide
    - Small group sizes
    - Transportation from Reykjavik
    - Duration: Approximately 3-4 hours.
    - Website: [Extreme Iceland](https://www.extremeiceland.is)

Booking Tips

- Book in Advance: Snorkeling tours can fill up quickly, especially during peak seasons (June to September). It's best to reserve your spot ahead of time.
    - Check Reviews: Look for reviews on platforms like TripAdvisor or Google to get an idea of the experiences from other travelers.
    - Verify Equipment: Ensure the tour operator provides high-quality gear, including drysuits suitable for cold-water conditions.

Northern Lights in Reykjavik, Iceland

Overview:

The Northern Lights, or Aurora Borealis, are a breathtaking natural phenomenon that attracts travelers to Iceland each year. These colorful displays of light in the night sky are caused by the interaction between charged particles from the sun and the Earth's magnetic field, resulting in beautiful waves of color, primarily greens, purples, and pinks.

—-

Best Time to See the Northern Lights

- Season: The Northern Lights are typically visible from late September to early April. The best chances for viewing occur during the winter months when the nights are longest and darkest.

- Peak Months: October, February, and March often provide optimal viewing conditions due to clearer skies and increased solar activity.

Ideal Viewing Conditions

- Dark Skies: The best views of the Northern Lights occur away from city lights. While Reykjavik has some viewing locations, it's advisable to venture further into the countryside for optimal experiences.
  - Weather: Clear, cloudless skies are essential for seeing the auroras. Check local weather forecasts and aurora forecasts (available online) to plan your viewing night.
  - Solar Activity: Increased solar activity enhances your chances of seeing stronger auroral displays. Various websites provide aurora forecasts based on solar activity levels.

Best Viewing Locations in and Around Reykjavik

1. Reykjavik City

- Perlan: Offers a great vantage point over the city, with minimal light pollution. The surrounding hills also provide a good backdrop.
  - Grótta Lighthouse: Located on the Seltjarnarnes Peninsula, this area is only a short drive from downtown and has dark skies ideal for Northern Lights viewing.

2. Þingvellir National Park

- Overview: A UNESCO World Heritage Site located about 45 minutes from Reykjavik, it offers stunning landscapes and dark skies away from urban light pollution.
 - Access: Accessible by car or through guided tours, making it a popular choice for aurora seekers.

3. Kirkjufell Mountain

- Overview: Located on the Snæfellsnes Peninsula, this iconic mountain provides a picturesque foreground for photography alongside the Northern Lights.
 - Travel: A longer drive from Reykjavik (about 2 hours), but the views are breathtaking.

4. Heiðmörk Nature Reserve

- Overview: Close to the city, this nature reserve offers several spots for viewing the auroras without straying too far from Reykjavik.
 - Access: Easily reachable by car and offers dark areas away from the city lights.

5. Þingvallavatn Lake

- Overview: This beautiful lake, located within Þingvellir National Park, offers fantastic reflections of the Northern Lights when the conditions are right.

- Experience: A scenic and serene spot, ideal for photography.

Northern Lights Tours

1. Guided Northern Lights Tours

- Overview: Many companies in Reykjavik offer guided tours specifically for Northern Lights viewing. These tours typically include transportation to optimal viewing locations.
   - Inclusions: Most tours provide warm clothing, snacks, and knowledgeable guides who can explain the science behind the phenomenon.

2. Photography Tours

- Overview: These specialized tours cater to photography enthusiasts, providing guidance on capturing the best images of the Northern Lights.
   - Inclusions: Photographers often use tripods and provide assistance with camera settings.

3. Boat Tours

- Overview: Some operators offer Northern Lights boat tours, providing a unique perspective from the water.
   - Experience: The absence of light pollution on the water can enhance visibility.

Tips for Viewing the Northern Lights

- Dress Warmly: Winter nights in Iceland can be extremely cold. Layer your clothing and wear insulated boots, hats, gloves, and scarves to stay warm while waiting for the lights to appear.
  - Be Patient: The Northern Lights can be unpredictable. It may take time for them to appear, so be prepared for a wait.
  - Check Aurora Forecasts: Websites and apps provide aurora forecasts that predict the likelihood of seeing the lights. Use these resources to plan your viewing.
  - Take a Camera: Capture the moment by bringing a camera with manual settings. A tripod is essential for long exposure shots.

Best Locations for Viewing the Northern Lights in Reykjavik, Iceland

Here's a list of some of the best locations around Reykjavik for experiencing the magical Northern Lights, along with tips on accessibility and what makes each spot unique.

1. Grótta Lighthouse

- Location: On the Seltjarnarnes Peninsula, a short drive or bus ride from downtown Reykjavik.
  - Why It's Great: Offers a stunning view of the lights over the ocean. The lighthouse adds a picturesque element to photos.

- Accessibility: Easily reachable by car or public transport; parking is available nearby.

2. Perlan

- Location: A landmark building in Reykjavik, situated on Öskjuhlíð Hill.
 - Why It's Great: Offers panoramic views of the city and surrounding areas. The elevated location helps minimize light pollution.
 - Accessibility: Open to the public; access to the viewing deck is available for a small fee.

3. Þingvellir National Park

- Location: About 45 minutes from Reykjavik.
 - Why It's Great: A UNESCO World Heritage Site with expansive dark skies and stunning landscapes, making it perfect for Northern Lights viewing.
 - Accessibility: Easily accessible by car or through guided tours; the park has several parking areas.

4. Heiðmörk Nature Reserve

- Location: Just outside Reykjavik.
 - Why It's Great: A natural area with minimal light pollution, providing various trails and clear views of the night sky.
 - Accessibility: Reachable by car; several parking areas are available.

5. Kirkjufell Mountain

- Location: On the Snæfellsnes Peninsula, about 2 hours from Reykjavik.
  - Why It's Great: This iconic mountain is a favorite for photographers, especially with the Northern Lights in the background.
  - Accessibility: Requires a drive, but the scenic route is worth it; parking is available near the mountain.

6. Þingvallavatn Lake

- Location: Within Þingvellir National Park.
  - Why It's Great: The lake can provide beautiful reflections of the Northern Lights, adding depth to your photographs.
  - Accessibility: Accessible by car; ensure you check the weather and road conditions.

7. Borgarnes

- Location: About 1 hour from Reykjavik.
  - Why It's Great: This small town provides access to dark areas with views of the Northern Lights over the fjord.
  - Accessibility: Easily reachable by car; several spots along the coast are perfect for viewing.

8. Laugarvatn

- Location: About 1 hour from Reykjavik, near the Golden Circle route.
 - Why It's Great: Offers dark skies and the possibility of viewing the lights reflected in the lake.
 - Accessibility: Accessible by car; parking is available near the lake.

9. Hellisheiði Geothermal Power Plant

- Location: About 30 minutes from Reykjavik.
 - Why It's Great: The surrounding area offers clear skies and beautiful landscapes for aurora viewing.
 - Accessibility: Reachable by car; parking is available.

10. Reykjanes Peninsula

- Location: Southwest of Reykjavik, around 45 minutes away.
 - Why It's Great: This area features diverse landscapes, geothermal activity, and fewer lights, making it a great spot for viewing the auroras.
 - Accessibility: Easily accessible by car; various lookout points along the coast.

Tips for Maximizing Your Viewing Experience

- Check the Aurora Forecast: Websites like the Icelandic Meteorological Office provide real-time aurora forecasts, helping you choose the best nights.

- Bring Warm Clothing: Dress in layers, as winter nights can be very cold. Bring hats, gloves, and insulated boots.

- Be Patient: The Northern Lights can be unpredictable; allow yourself enough time to wait for the display.

- Stay Away from City Lights: The darker the area, the better your chances of seeing the auroras. If possible, travel at least 30 minutes outside Reykjavik.

Tips for Photographing the Northern Lights (Aurora Borealis)

Capturing the mesmerizing beauty of the Northern Lights requires some knowledge of night photography and preparation. Here are detailed tips to help you get the best possible shots:

1. Use a DSLR or Mirrorless Camera

- Why: These cameras allow you to manually adjust settings such as shutter speed, aperture, and ISO, which are crucial for night photography. Compact cameras and smartphones often struggle to capture the detail and vibrancy of the auroras.

2. Bring a Sturdy Tripod

- Why: Long exposure photography requires the camera to remain perfectly still. A tripod will help avoid any motion blur, ensuring sharp images.

3. Use a Wide-Angle Lens

- Why: A wide-angle lens (14-24mm) captures more of the sky, allowing you to include both the auroras and the surrounding landscape for a more dramatic shot.
    - Aperture: Choose a lens with a fast aperture (f/2.8 or lower) to let in more light during night photography.

4. Shoot in RAW Format

- Why: RAW files preserve much more detail than JPEGs, especially in low-light conditions. This gives you more flexibility when editing your photos, such as adjusting exposure and color balance without losing quality.

5. Set Manual Focus

- Why: Autofocus often fails in low-light conditions, so manually focus on a distant light source (such as a bright star or a distant building). You can also set your lens focus to infinity for sharper results.

6. Adjust ISO Settings

- ISO 800–3200: Start with ISO 800 and adjust higher (up to 3200) depending on how much light is available and how strong the aurora display is. Keep in mind that higher ISO settings increase sensitivity but may introduce noise into the image.

7. Set Shutter Speed

- Shutter speed 5–20 seconds: Use a longer exposure time (5-20 seconds) to capture enough light and the movement of the auroras. If the auroras are very active and moving quickly, you may want to use a shorter shutter speed (e.g., 5-10 seconds) to avoid overexposing the light.

8. Adjust Aperture

- Wide Aperture (f/2.8 - f/4): Set your aperture to the lowest number possible (f/2.8 or f/3.5) to allow as much light as possible into the camera. A wider aperture helps you capture the faint aurora lights and the night sky without having to increase the ISO too much.

9. Set a Low White Balance

- 2500K–4000K: Adjust the white balance to a lower Kelvin (K) temperature, between 2500K and 4000K. This helps capture the natural colors of the Northern Lights without them looking too warm or yellowish.

10. Use a Remote Shutter Release or Timer

- Why: Using a remote or setting a timer (2-5 seconds) prevents camera shake from pressing the shutter button, resulting in sharper images.

11. Compose Your Shot

- Foreground Elements: Include a compelling foreground like mountains, lakes, trees, or buildings (such as Grótta Lighthouse or Kirkjufell Mountain) to give context and depth to your images. The contrast between the still foreground and the dynamic auroras creates a more striking composition.
  - Rule of Thirds: Use the rule of thirds to place the horizon or aurora at key points in your composition for a balanced image.

12. Experiment with Exposure Times

- Try Different Durations: Start with a 5-10 second exposure and adjust based on the strength and speed of the aurora. For fast-moving auroras, shorter exposures will capture the detail of the lights without them becoming too blurred.

13. Be Patient and Prepared

- Patience is Key: The auroras can be unpredictable and may fade or intensify. Be prepared to wait for the right moment.
  - Warm Gear: Since you may be outdoors in freezing conditions for extended periods, dress warmly in layers, bring gloves, and pack extra batteries (cold temperatures drain them faster).

14. Practice Beforehand

- Night Photography Practice: Before heading out, practice shooting in low-light conditions and familiarize yourself with your camera's manual settings. This will help you adjust quickly when the Northern Lights appear.

15. Post-Processing

- Edit Carefully: When editing your images, adjust the contrast and exposure to bring out the details of the auroras without over-editing. Tools like Lightroom or Photoshop can help fine-tune the final image, but try to maintain the natural look of the auroras.

Summary of Settings for Northern Lights Photography:

- Camera Mode: Manual
    - ISO: 800–3200
    - Shutter Speed: 5–20 seconds
    - Aperture: f/2.8–f/4
    - Focus: Manual, set to infinity
    - White Balance: 2500K–4000K
    - Lens: Wide-angle, fast aperture

By following these tips and experimenting with your camera settings, you'll be well-prepared to capture the incredible beauty of the Northern

Lights in Reykjavik.

Local Cuisine and Dining

Traditional Icelandic Dishes

Icelandic cuisine is deeply rooted in the island's history, culture, and geography, featuring dishes that reflect its reliance on the surrounding ocean, fertile lands, and age-old preservation methods. Here's a look at some must-try traditional Icelandic dishes when visiting Reykjavik:

1. Hákarl (Fermented Shark)

- What: This iconic dish is made from Greenland shark that has been fermented and hung to dry for several months. Known for its strong, ammonia-like taste and smell, it's often considered an adventurous food for tourists but is part of Iceland's culinary heritage.
  - Where to Try: Many local restaurants offer small bites of hákarl, and it's often served with a shot of Brennivín (Icelandic schnapps).

2. Plokkfiskur (Fish Stew)

- What: A comforting dish made from boiled and mashed white fish, such as cod or haddock, mixed with potatoes, onions, butter, and milk. This hearty stew is a staple in Icelandic homes and is often served with dark rye bread.
    - Where to Try: Found in many cafes and family restaurants throughout Reykjavik.

3. Svið (Boiled Sheep's Head)

- What: A unique traditional dish made by boiling a whole sheep's head, often served split in half. The head is sometimes singed to remove fur, and it's eaten along with the brain, eyes, and tongue.
    - Where to Try: Available at traditional Icelandic restaurants, though considered more of a cultural experience for visitors.

4. Hangikjöt (Smoked Lamb)

- What: Smoked lamb or mutton, often served thinly sliced, either warm or cold. The lamb is typically smoked over birch wood, giving it a rich, distinct flavor. Hangikjöt is a common dish during festive seasons like Christmas.
    - Where to Try: Served in traditional eateries, especially during the holiday season.

5. Rúgbrauð (Icelandic Rye Bread)

- What: A dense, dark rye bread often baked in geothermal steam underground, giving it a sweet and slightly chewy texture. Rúgbrauð is commonly served with butter, smoked lamb, or fish dishes.
  - Where to Try: Available at many Reykjavik bakeries and restaurants; try it with butter and smoked salmon for a traditional Icelandic snack.

6. Pylsur (Icelandic Hot Dog)

- What: Icelandic hot dogs are made from a mix of lamb, pork, and beef, and are a beloved street food. They're usually topped with raw and fried onions, ketchup, sweet brown mustard, and a remoulade sauce.
  - Where to Try: The famous hot dog stand **Bæjarins Beztu Pylsur** in Reykjavik is a must-visit for an authentic Icelandic hot dog experience.

7. Kjötsúpa (Icelandic Lamb Soup)

- What: A hearty and traditional soup made from lamb, root vegetables (such as potatoes, carrots, and turnips), and herbs. It's slow-cooked to create a flavorful broth, and is perfect for warming up on cold Icelandic days.
  - Where to Try: Many local restaurants and family kitchens serve this comforting soup, particularly during colder months.

8. Harðfiskur (Dried Fish)

- What: Dried fish, typically cod, haddock, or wolffish, is a popular snack in Iceland. It's often eaten with butter and can be enjoyed as a crunchy, protein-rich treat.
   - Where to Try: You can find harðfiskur in supermarkets and traditional food stores across Reykjavik.

9. Skyr (Icelandic Yogurt)

- What: Skyr is a creamy, high-protein dairy product that resembles yogurt but has a milder flavor and thicker texture. It's often served with berries, honey, or granola and is a popular breakfast or dessert option.
   - Where to Try: Found in grocery stores, cafes, and restaurants across Reykjavik. Skyr is available in various flavors, including traditional plain or with fruits.

10. Brennivín (Icelandic Schnapps)

- What: While not a dish, Brennivín is Iceland's signature schnapps, often referred to as "Black Death." It's a potent spirit made from fermented grain or potatoes and flavored with caraway seeds. Brennivín is traditionally paired with hákarl.
   - Where to Try: Available in most bars and restaurants in Reykjavik, especially when you want to pair it with traditional Icelandic dishes.

11. Flatkaka (Flatbread)

- What: A traditional unleavened rye flatbread, usually served warm and often paired with butter, smoked lamb, or fish.
  - Where to Try: You'll find flatkaka served alongside many Icelandic dishes in local restaurants or available in supermarkets.

12. Icelandic Fish and Chips

- What: While not as traditional as other dishes, Iceland's version of fish and chips typically uses fresh, local cod or haddock and serves it with a twist—batter made from spelt flour and a dipping sauce made from skyr.
  - Where to Try: Icelandic Fish & Chips restaurant in Reykjavik is known for its fresh, healthier take on this classic dish.

Exploring Iceland's culinary landscape gives visitors a deeper connection to the island's traditions, with its reliance on simple, locally sourced ingredients. Don't miss these traditional dishes during your visit to Reykjavik!

Fermented Shark (Hákarl)

Hákarl is one of Iceland's most infamous traditional dishes, known for its strong and distinct taste. This delicacy is made from the Greenland shark, a species that contains high levels of toxins when fresh. As a result, it undergoes a unique fermentation and drying process that has been passed down through Icelandic history.

Preparation Process:

- Fermentation: To prepare hákarl, the shark's meat is first buried in gravel or placed in a shallow pit to ferment for 6-12 weeks. This allows the meat to release harmful toxins.
 - Drying: After fermentation, the meat is hung to dry in open-air sheds for several months, where it develops a hard, leathery exterior. The inner flesh becomes soft and develops its pungent smell.

Taste and Experience:

- Taste: Hákarl has a strong ammonia-like odor that can be off-putting to many. Its taste is intense, often described as fishy and tangy, with a chewy texture.
 - How It's Served: It's typically served in small, cubed pieces as an appetizer and traditionally paired with a shot of Brennivín, Iceland's signature schnapps, to wash down the strong flavors.

Cultural Significance:

- Hákarl dates back to a time when preserving food was essential for survival in Iceland's harsh environment. It represents Iceland's resourcefulness and the preservation methods used in traditional Icelandic cuisine.

Where to Try:

- Many traditional Icelandic restaurants in Reykjavik offer hákarl as part of tasting menus or as a small appetizer. Visitors can try it at places such as Café Loki and Kolaportið (Reykjavik's flea market), where it is sold as small bites.

For the adventurous traveler, tasting hákarl is an unforgettable culinary experience that connects you to Iceland's rugged history and traditions.

Lamb Soup (Kjötsúpa)

Kjötsúpa is a traditional Icelandic lamb soup, deeply rooted in the country's culture and history. This hearty dish has been a staple in Icelandic homes for centuries, often enjoyed during the colder months. It's known for its simplicity, wholesome ingredients, and rich flavor, making it a comfort food for locals and visitors alike.

Ingredients:

- Lamb: The star of the dish is lamb, often on the bone for added flavor. Icelandic lamb is known for its high quality, as the animals graze freely on the country's natural, unspoiled pastures.
    - Root Vegetables: Typical vegetables include potatoes, carrots, rutabagas (swedes), and onions, all of which grow well in Iceland's climate.
    - Herbs: Traditional Icelandic herbs like thyme and bay leaves are used for seasoning, adding earthy notes to the broth.

- Barley or Rice (optional): Sometimes grains like barley or rice are added to make the soup even more filling.

Preparation:

- The lamb is simmered with water and herbs to create a rich broth.
- Once the lamb is partially cooked, vegetables are added and slow-cooked together until tender.
- The result is a flavorful, nutrient-dense soup, perfect for warming up on a chilly day.

Taste and Experience:

- Flavor: The soup has a delicate yet rich flavor, with the lamb providing a deep, meaty base complemented by the sweetness of the root vegetables.
- Texture: The slow-cooked lamb becomes tender, and the vegetables soften, creating a satisfying, homely meal that's easy to enjoy.

Cultural Significance:

- Kjötsúpa has been part of Icelandic cuisine for generations. It's considered a traditional dish passed down through families, often eaten during large gatherings or on special occasions like festivals and holidays.
- It reflects the Icelandic way of making the most of simple, local ingredients to create something hearty and delicious.

Where to Try:

- Lækjarbrekka and Café Loki are popular spots in Reykjavik where visitors can enjoy a bowl of traditional kjötsúpa.
    - During winter festivals or local food markets, you can also find lamb soup being served as a seasonal specialty.

Best Time to Eat:

- Kjötsúpa is particularly comforting during the colder months, making it a perfect dish for autumn and winter. However, it's available year-round in many restaurants in Reykjavik.

A bowl of kjötsúpa offers not just sustenance but also a taste of Iceland's culinary heritage. It's an authentic dish that represents the Icelandic way of life: simple, hearty, and grounded in nature.

Skyr

Skyr is a traditional Icelandic dairy product that has been enjoyed for over a thousand years. Though it resembles yogurt, skyr is technically a type of cheese. It is prized for its creamy texture, high protein content, and slightly tangy flavor, making it a popular and healthy snack in Iceland and beyond.

What is Skyr?:

- Texture: Skyr is thick and creamy, similar to Greek yogurt but slightly denser.
    - Taste: It has a mild, slightly sour taste with a hint of natural sweetness. It can be enjoyed plain or flavored with fruits like berries or vanilla.
    - Nutritional Benefits: Skyr is rich in protein and low in fat, making it a nutritious option for a light meal or snack.

How Skyr is Made:

- Milk: Skyr is made from skimmed milk that is cultured with live bacteria and then strained to remove the whey, resulting in a thick, creamy texture.
    - Traditional Method: Historically, skyr was produced by fermenting raw milk, but modern versions are pasteurized and often mass-produced.
    - Natural Sweetener: While plain skyr has a tart flavor, many commercial versions are sweetened or mixed with fruit to appeal to a wider range of tastes.

How to Enjoy Skyr:

- Plain: Traditionally, skyr is eaten plain with a drizzle of honey or cream.
    - Toppings: Many Icelanders add fresh berries, nuts, or granola for extra texture and flavor.
    - In Recipes: Skyr can be used in smoothies, desserts, or as a substitute

for sour cream in savory dishes.

Cultural Significance:

- Skyr has been a part of Icelandic culture since the Viking era, making it an iconic symbol of Icelandic heritage. It was originally used as a preserved food source in the harsh Icelandic climate and has remained a staple ever since.
   - Today, it is embraced by both locals and visitors for its nutritional value and versatility.

Where to Try:

- Skyr is widely available in supermarkets and cafes throughout Iceland. You can find both plain and flavored varieties, including blueberry, strawberry, and vanilla.
   - For a more artisanal experience, you can try freshly made skyr at local farms or specialized dairy shops around Reykjavik.

Popular Brands:

- Some well-known Icelandic skyr brands include MS Skyr and Ísey Skyr, which are also exported internationally, making skyr a global sensation.

Modern Skyr Trends:

- Skyr has gained popularity in other countries as a healthy alternative to yogurt. Its high protein content and low fat have made it a favorite among fitness enthusiasts.

Whether you enjoy it as part of a traditional Icelandic breakfast or as a modern twist in smoothies or desserts, skyr offers a delicious and nutritious taste of Icelandic culture.

Recommended Restaurants and Cafes in Reykjavik

Reykjavik offers a wide range of dining options that reflect both its traditional Icelandic roots and international influences. Whether you're looking to try authentic Icelandic dishes or enjoy a casual coffee, the city's vibrant food scene has something for every traveler.

Traditional Icelandic Cuisine:

1. Dill Restaurant

- Cuisine: Modern Icelandic, Michelin-starred
    - Location: Laugavegur
    - Overview: Dill is Reykjavik's premier fine-dining establishment, known for its innovative takes on traditional Icelandic ingredients. The restaurant uses local, seasonal produce to create exquisite tasting menus featuring dishes like Icelandic lamb, Arctic char, and foraged herbs. The ambiance is minimalist, focusing on the food's natural flavors and

presentation.

2. Matur og Drykkur

- Cuisine: Traditional Icelandic
    - Location: Grandagarður
    - Overview: A highly recommended spot for those looking to experience authentic Icelandic flavors with a modern twist. Matur og Drykkur offers dishes like fish stew, fermented shark (hákarl), and lamb in a cozy yet contemporary setting. Their dedication to reviving old Icelandic recipes makes it a culinary destination for food enthusiasts.

3. Café Loki
    - Cuisine: Casual Icelandic
    - Location: Across from Hallgrimskirkja
    - Overview: Café Loki offers a taste of traditional Icelandic dishes like lamb soup (kjötsúpa), rye bread ice cream, and platters featuring dried fish, smoked lamb, and hákarl. The café's location near the Hallgrimskirkja church provides stunning views and a warm, welcoming atmosphere.

Seafood Restaurants:

1. Fiskmarkaðurinn (The Fish Market)

- Cuisine: Icelandic Seafood
    - Location: Aðalstræti
    - Overview: A seafood lover's paradise, The Fish Market offers fresh, locally caught fish and shellfish prepared with Asian-inspired flavors.

Popular dishes include langoustine tempura, sushi made from Icelandic fish, and charred salmon. The restaurant's sleek and stylish décor adds to the upscale dining experience.

2. Sægreifinn (The Sea Baron)

- Cuisine: Seafood, Casual Dining
  - Location: Geirsgata, Old Harbor
  - Overview: This casual harborside restaurant is famous for its lobster soup and fresh seafood skewers, including whale, shrimp, and cod. The rustic, maritime-themed interior adds to the charm, making it a favorite among both tourists and locals.

International and Contemporary Dining:

1. Apotek Restaurant

- Cuisine: Contemporary Icelandic with International Flair
  - Location: Austurstræti
  - Overview: Housed in a historic former pharmacy, Apotek offers an eclectic mix of Icelandic and international cuisine. Known for its fusion dishes and excellent cocktails, it's perfect for a relaxed yet sophisticated dining experience. Popular items include Icelandic lamb and seafood dishes alongside international flavors.

2. Snaps Bistro Bar

- Cuisine: French-Inspired Bistro
  - Location: Þórsgata
  - Overview: Snaps is a chic, cozy French bistro serving classics like steak frites, moules marinières, and tartare, but with an Icelandic twist using local ingredients. It's a popular spot for brunch and dinner, offering a laid-back yet stylish atmosphere.

Cafes and Coffeehouses:

1. Reykjavik Roasters

- Cuisine: Coffeehouse
  - Location: Kárastígur & Brautarholt
  - Overview: For coffee lovers, Reykjavik Roasters is a must-visit. It's known for its carefully sourced beans and excellent brews. The cozy, rustic décor and relaxed vibe make it a great place to take a break after exploring the city. They also offer pastries and light snacks.

2. Sandholt Bakery

- Cuisine: Bakery and Café
  - Location: Laugavegur
  - Overview: Sandholt is one of Reykjavik's most beloved bakeries, offering a variety of fresh pastries, breads, and sandwiches. Popular items include their sourdough bread, cinnamon rolls, and pastries with Icelandic berries. The bakery also serves coffee, making it a perfect breakfast or snack stop.

3. Kaffivagninn

- Cuisine: Café, Casual Dining
  - Location: Old Harbor
  - Overview: Reykjavik's oldest café, Kaffivagninn, is a charming and historic spot right by the harbor. It's an ideal place to enjoy a cup of coffee or tea while watching the boats. They serve hearty breakfasts, soups, and seafood dishes, making it a great stop for any time of the day.

Vegetarian and Vegan Options:

1. Gló

- Cuisine: Healthy, Vegetarian, Vegan
  - Location: Laugavegur
  - Overview: Gló offers a variety of healthy, plant-based meals using fresh, organic ingredients. The menu includes salads, vegan bowls, and gluten-free dishes, making it a great option for health-conscious travelers. They also offer fish and chicken for those who prefer non-vegetarian options.

2. Kröst

- Cuisine: Vegetarian-friendly, Local Produce
  - Location: Hlemmur Mathöll (Food Hall)
  - Overview: Located in the trendy Hlemmur food hall, Kröst focuses on fresh, seasonal ingredients. Their menu is diverse, offering a mix of vegetarian and meat options, with an emphasis on local produce and

artisanal preparations.

Reykjavik's culinary scene offers something for everyone, from traditional Icelandic fare to contemporary fusion dishes and global flavors. Whether you're looking for a quick snack, a cozy café, or an unforgettable dining experience, these recommended restaurants and cafes will give you a true taste of Reykjavik's vibrant food culture.

Top Dining Spots in Reykjavik

Reykjavik's dining scene is known for its mix of traditional Icelandic dishes and innovative international cuisine. Here are some of the top restaurants and dining experiences to try when visiting the city.

1. Dill Restaurant

- Cuisine: Modern Icelandic (Michelin-starred)
  - Location: Laugavegur
  - Overview: As the first Michelin-starred restaurant in Iceland, Dill is renowned for its creative approach to Icelandic ingredients. With a focus on local and seasonal produce, the tasting menus offer unique dishes such as Icelandic lamb, Arctic char, and foraged herbs. The minimalist and elegant ambiance complements the artistic presentation of the food.

LOCAL CUISINE AND DINING

2. Fiskmarkaðurinn (The Fish Market)

- Cuisine: Icelandic Seafood
    - Location: Aðalstræti, near Reykjavik Harbor
    - Overview: The Fish Market is a must-visit for seafood lovers, offering a blend of Icelandic seafood with Asian-inspired flavors. The menu includes sushi, sashimi, and Icelandic classics like langoustine and cod, along with grilled meat. The contemporary setting is stylish and ideal for an upscale dining experience.

3. Matur og Drykkur

- Cuisine: Traditional Icelandic
    - Location: Grandagarður
    - Overview: This restaurant is dedicated to reviving old Icelandic recipes with a modern twist. Popular dishes include fish stew, fermented shark (hákarl), and Icelandic lamb, all served in a cozy yet modern environment. Matur og Drykkur is a great choice for anyone looking to try authentic Icelandic dishes in a contemporary setting.

4. Grillmarkaðurinn (The Grill Market)

- Cuisine: Icelandic Grill
    - Location: Lækjargata
    - Overview: Known for its farm-to-table philosophy, The Grill Market specializes in grilled Icelandic meats like lamb, beef, and puffin, along with a variety of seafood options. The rustic interior, complete with lava rock and wood accents, provides a warm and inviting atmosphere for a refined yet hearty dining experience.

5. Sægreifinn (The Sea Baron)

- Cuisine: Casual Seafood
  - Location: Reykjavik Harbor
  - Overview: This charming, no-frills restaurant is famous for its lobster soup and seafood skewers, including whale, shrimp, and cod. Located by the old harbor, Sægreifinn offers a casual atmosphere with a maritime theme. It's a local favorite for those seeking fresh, affordable seafood in an informal setting.

6. Apotek Restaurant

- Cuisine: Contemporary Icelandic with International Influences
  - Location: Austurstræti
  - Overview: Housed in a historic former pharmacy, Apotek offers an eclectic menu blending Icelandic ingredients with international flavors. The restaurant is known for its sophisticated yet welcoming atmosphere, offering dishes like slow-cooked lamb, seafood, and inventive cocktails. It's a great spot for a special night out.

7. Snaps Bistro

- Cuisine: French Bistro with Icelandic Ingredients
  - Location: Þórsgata
  - Overview: A popular spot for locals and visitors alike, Snaps offers a French-inspired menu with an Icelandic twist. Think moules frites, steak tartare, and fresh seafood. The bistro has a cozy, lively atmosphere and is a favorite for brunch and dinner.

8. Kopar

- Cuisine: Seafood and Seasonal Dishes
  - Location: Reykjavik Old Harbor
  - Overview: Set in a charming harbor-front location, Kopar serves dishes inspired by the sea and the seasons. The restaurant focuses on Icelandic seafood such as langoustine, mussels, and scallops, with an emphasis on fresh and sustainable ingredients. The view of the harbor adds to the dining experience.

9. Hlemmur Mathöll (Food Hall)

- Cuisine: Various (International and Icelandic Street Food)
  - Location: Hlemmur Square
  - Overview: Hlemmur Mathöll is a modern food hall offering a wide range of dining options, from gourmet hot dogs and burgers to vegan dishes and freshly baked pastries. It's the perfect place to sample a variety of flavors in one spot, ideal for a casual meal or snack while exploring the city.

10. Skál! at Hlemmur Mathöll

- Cuisine: New Nordic Cuisine, Small Plates
  - Location: Hlemmur Mathöll
  - Overview: Skál! is a trendy spot in the Hlemmur food hall, offering modern Nordic cuisine with an emphasis on sharing plates. Using locally sourced ingredients, the menu includes small dishes like lamb ribs, pickled vegetables, and unique fermented foods, giving diners a taste of contemporary Icelandic cuisine in a laid-back atmosphere.

Reykjavik's top dining spots offer everything from fine dining and traditional Icelandic dishes to casual seafood joints and international fare. Whether you're looking for a Michelin-starred experience or a quick bite by the harbor, these recommendations provide a comprehensive guide to enjoying the best of Reykjavik's culinary scene.

Local Food Markets in Reykjavik

Exploring local food markets in Reykjavik is a great way to experience Icelandic culture, sample fresh produce, and discover unique regional delicacies. Here are some of the best food markets to visit during your stay:

1. Kolaportið Flea Market

- Location: Tryggvagata, near Reykjavik Harbor
  - Hours: Open weekends (Saturday & Sunday), 11:00 AM - 5:00 PM
  - Overview: Kolaportið is Reykjavik's largest and most famous indoor flea market, offering a wide variety of goods, including fresh seafood, traditional Icelandic food, second-hand clothing, books, antiques, and more. This market is a great place to try hákarl (fermented shark), harðfiskur (dried fish), and other traditional Icelandic products. The seafood section also offers fresh fish, and there are plenty of stalls selling Icelandic pastries, candy, and snacks.

2. Hlemmur Mathöll (Food Hall)

- Location: Hlemmur Square
  - Hours: Open daily, 10:00 AM - 10:00 PM
  - Overview: Hlemmur Mathöll is a trendy food hall located in a former bus terminal, offering a variety of food stalls featuring both Icelandic and international cuisine. You can find artisanal bread, freshly brewed coffee, ice cream, seafood, and vegan dishes, as well as locally sourced produce. While it's more of a modern food court than a traditional market, it's a fantastic place to taste local flavors and meet local food producers.

3. Reykjavik Farmers Market

- Location: Laugavegur, central Reykjavik
  - Overview: Reykjavik Farmers Market is a seasonal market that appears at various locations during the summer and special events. Farmers and producers from all over Iceland bring fresh fruits, vegetables, dairy products, and meats. You can also find homemade jams, honey, and craft beverages. It's a great place to sample Icelandic farm-to-table ingredients and chat with local farmers about their products.

4. Melabúðin

- Location: Hagamelur, Vesturbær neighborhood
  - Overview: Melabúðin is a beloved local grocery store with a reputation for offering high-quality Icelandic products, including fresh fish, lamb, dairy, and baked goods. While it's a regular supermarket, it's known for its excellent selection of local Icelandic delicacies and

fresh produce, making it a popular spot for locals and visitors alike to experience authentic Icelandic groceries.

5. Fjarðarkaup

- Location: Hafnarfjörður, Greater Reykjavik Area
   - Overview: Located in Hafnarfjörður, a short drive from Reykjavik, Fjarðarkaup is a large supermarket offering a variety of Icelandic products, from fresh seafood to meat and dairy. The store also features organic Icelandic vegetables and fruits. Fjarðarkaup is a good option if you want to shop for local groceries in a quieter, more residential setting.

6. Brauð & Co.

- Location: Multiple locations around Reykjavik (Frakkastígur, Laugavegur, etc.)
   - Overview: Though not a market, Brauð & Co. is Reykjavik's most famous bakery, known for its artisan bread and pastries made from locally sourced ingredients. This bakery is the go-to spot for locals looking for freshly baked goods like cinnamon buns (kanilsnúðar), sourdough bread, and rye bread (rúgbrauð), a staple of Icelandic cuisine. Stop by to pick up some treats made with traditional Icelandic methods.

Reykjavik's food markets and gourmet halls offer an authentic glimpse into Icelandic culinary traditions. From seafood and fermented foods at Kolaportið to modern flavors at Hlemmur Mathöll, these local markets provide a unique taste of Reykjavik's vibrant food culture.

Food Tours and Culinary Experiences in Reykjavik

Reykjavik offers a variety of food tours and culinary experiences that allow visitors to explore the flavors and traditions of Icelandic cuisine. From guided food walks through the city to immersive hands-on cooking classes, these tours provide a deep dive into Iceland's unique food culture.

1. Reykjavik Food Walk

- Overview: One of the most popular food tours in Reykjavik, the Reykjavik Food Walk takes you on a guided tour through the heart of the city, visiting local restaurants, cafes, and food stalls. You'll get to sample iconic Icelandic dishes like lamb soup (kjötsúpa), freshly caught seafood, and traditional desserts like Icelandic rye bread. Along the way, the knowledgeable guides provide insights into Icelandic history, culture, and culinary traditions.
  - Highlights:
  - Taste Icelandic classics such as hákarl (fermented shark) and plokkfiskur (fish stew)
  - Explore Reykjavik's charming streets and hidden food gems
  - Learn about the local food culture from expert guides

2. Icelandic Gourmet Feast

- Overview: This gourmet dining experience offers a multi-course tasting menu at a high-end Reykjavik restaurant, where you can enjoy a curated selection of Icelandic delicacies. The menu often includes

specialties like Arctic char, lamb, langoustine, and traditional Icelandic desserts. It's an excellent way to experience the finest in Icelandic cuisine with a focus on fresh, seasonal, and locally sourced ingredients.
  - Highlights:
  - Multi-course dinner featuring Icelandic ingredients
  - Fine dining experience in one of Reykjavik's top restaurants
  - Option to pair with local wines or craft beers

3. Reykjavik Beer and Food Tour

- Overview: Combining Iceland's growing craft beer scene with traditional food, this tour takes you to some of the best bars and microbreweries in Reykjavik. You'll get to sample local brews alongside classic Icelandic bar food, such as smoked lamb, fish, and cheeses. This is a great option for those interested in tasting Icelandic beer culture while enjoying hearty food.
  - Highlights:
  - Visit popular Reykjavik bars and breweries
  - Sample a variety of Icelandic craft beers and ales
  - Enjoy Icelandic pub snacks like dried fish (harðfiskur) and cured meats

4. Reykjavik Street Food Tour

- Overview: For a more casual and accessible food tour, the Reykjavik Street Food Tour offers a taste of Iceland's street food scene. You'll visit local food trucks and street vendors, trying dishes like fish and chips, Icelandic hot dogs (pylsur), and kleina (Icelandic donuts). This tour offers an affordable and fun way to sample everyday Icelandic food,

often in outdoor settings.
  - Highlights:
  - Taste the iconic Icelandic hot dog at the famous Bæjarins Beztu Pylsur stand
    - Sample local seafood from food trucks and vendors
    - Explore Reykjavik's street food culture

5. Traditional Icelandic Cooking Class

- Overview: For those looking to immerse themselves in the culinary arts, a traditional Icelandic cooking class is a perfect hands-on experience. These classes often take place in small, intimate settings where you'll learn to prepare dishes like Icelandic fish soup, rye bread, and skyr-based desserts under the guidance of a local chef. The class typically ends with a communal meal where participants can enjoy the fruits of their labor.
  - Highlights:
  - Learn to cook classic Icelandic dishes with a local chef
  - Discover the traditional methods of baking and preserving
  - Enjoy a homemade meal at the end of the class

6. Northern Lights and Dinner Tour

- Overview: This unique experience combines two of Iceland's highlights—northern lights viewing and Icelandic cuisine. The evening begins with a traditional Icelandic dinner, often served at a countryside restaurant or guesthouse. Afterward, you'll be taken to a dark-sky location to witness the Aurora Borealis. This tour is a great option for those wanting to combine the culinary and natural wonders of Iceland

in one memorable evening.
- Highlights:
- Enjoy a traditional Icelandic dinner before the northern lights tour
- Local dishes often include fish, lamb, and seasonal vegetables
- Chance to view the stunning Aurora Borealis

7. Private Seafood Dining Experience

- Overview: For seafood lovers, this exclusive dining experience focuses on Iceland's fresh fish and shellfish. Hosted in either a Reykjavik restaurant or private setting, you'll get a multi-course meal featuring Icelandic favorites like Arctic char, langoustine, and cod. Some tours even offer the chance to meet the fishermen and learn about sustainable fishing practices in Iceland.
- Highlights:
- Taste the freshest seafood Iceland has to offer
- Learn about local fishing practices and sustainability
- Private dining experience with a focus on Icelandic ocean cuisine

Why Choose a Culinary Experience in Reykjavik?

Icelandic cuisine is shaped by the country's harsh climate, unique geography, and rich cultural history. Food tours and culinary experiences in Reykjavik allow visitors to not only taste traditional Icelandic dishes but also understand their significance in Icelandic culture. Whether you're sampling fermented shark or enjoying gourmet seafood, these experiences offer a delicious journey into Iceland's food heritage.

Accommodations

Where to Stay in Reykjavik

Reykjavik offers a diverse range of accommodations that cater to various tastes and budgets, from luxurious hotels to cozy guesthouses and budget-friendly hostels. Below are some of the best neighborhoods to stay in and recommendations for different types of travelers.

1. Downtown Reykjavik (Miðborg)

- Overview: The heart of Reykjavik, Miðborg, is the most popular area for visitors to stay in due to its central location. It's home to most of the city's key attractions, such as Hallgrimskirkja, Harpa Concert Hall, Laugavegur Street, and plenty of restaurants, cafes, and bars. Staying here allows you to explore much of Reykjavik on foot.
    - Best for: First-time visitors, those interested in nightlife, and travelers looking for convenience.

Top Hotels:

- Canopy by Hilton Reykjavik City Centre: A modern, stylish hotel located near Laugavegur Street, offering sleek rooms and a rooftop bar with great views.
  - Hotel Borg by Keahotels: A luxury option that combines art deco elegance with modern amenities, located near Austurvöllur Park.
  - Kvosin Downtown Hotel: A boutique hotel known for its chic interiors and spacious rooms, perfect for families or longer stays.

2. Vesturbær (West Town)

- Overview: Vesturbær is a quieter, more residential neighborhood just west of downtown. It's known for its proximity to Reykjavik's Old Harbour and attractions like the Saga Museum and the famous Vesturbæjarlaug swimming pool. This area provides a more relaxed atmosphere while still being close to the city center.
  - Best for: Travelers seeking a quieter, local experience and proximity to nature.

Top Hotels:

- Icelandair Hotel Reykjavik Marina: A quirky, nautically-themed hotel with views of the harbor and a lively bar.
  - Reykjavik Marina Residence: A luxurious, private option offering spacious suites with sea views, ideal for couples or small groups.

3. Laugardalur

- Overview: Laugardalur is Reykjavik's recreational hub, home to Laugardalslaug, the city's largest geothermal pool, and the botanical gardens. Though slightly outside the city center, it offers a peaceful environment and is perfect for families or those who want to enjoy outdoor activities. Public transport easily connects it to downtown.
  - Best for: Families, wellness seekers, and outdoor enthusiasts.

Top Hotels:

- Hilton Reykjavik Nordica: A sleek, upscale hotel offering a spa, restaurant, and easy access to both downtown and the recreational facilities in Laugardalur.
  - Grand Hotel Reykjavik: A large hotel with modern amenities, ideal for business travelers or families seeking comfort and convenience.

4. Hlemmur Square

- Overview: The area around Hlemmur Square is vibrant and offers a mix of modern and budget accommodations. It's close to the main bus terminal, making it convenient for day trips out of Reykjavik. The Hlemmur food hall is nearby, offering a range of local and international cuisine.
  - Best for: Budget travelers, solo travelers, and those looking for a lively area.

Top Accommodations:

- Hlemmur Square Hotel & Hostel: A great option for budget-conscious travelers, offering both hotel-style rooms and dormitory accommodations.
   - Storm Hotel by Keahotels: A contemporary hotel with simple yet comfortable rooms, just a short walk from downtown.

5. Old Harbour Area

- Overview: The Old Harbour area is perfect for those who want to be close to whale watching tours and other maritime activities. The area has seen recent development and now boasts some of Reykjavik's trendiest hotels, restaurants, and shops. It offers beautiful views of the bay and Mount Esja.
   - Best for: Families, couples, and travelers interested in marine tours.

Top Hotels:

- Exeter Hotel by Keahotels: A trendy, industrial-chic hotel with a great restaurant, located right by the harbor.
   - Black Pearl Apartments: Luxurious, fully equipped apartments with spacious living areas, perfect for families or extended stays.

6. Hlíðar

- Overview: Located to the east of the city center, Hlíðar is a peaceful, residential neighborhood that offers a more local experience. It's within walking distance of downtown Reykjavik and is well-connected by public transport. The area is home to some great museums and parks.
 - Best for: Budget travelers, those seeking a quieter stay, and long-term visitors.

Top Hotels:

- Reykjavik Lights by Keahotels: A stylish, affordable hotel with a light-themed decor and beautiful views of the city.
 - 101 Guesthouse: A no-frills, budget-friendly guesthouse that offers clean, comfortable rooms within easy walking distance of downtown.

Budget-Friendly Accommodations

For travelers on a tighter budget, Reykjavik offers a variety of hostels, guesthouses, and affordable hotels.

Best Options:

- Loft HI Hostel: A central, eco-friendly hostel with a rooftop terrace and a great social atmosphere.
 - Reykjavik Downtown HI Hostel: A budget-friendly option near the Old Harbour, offering both dormitory beds and private rooms.
 - Galaxy Pod Hostel: A unique, futuristic hostel with "pod" style beds,

offering privacy at a low cost.

Luxury Accommodations

For those seeking luxury, Reykjavik also offers some high-end options that provide top-notch service and amenities.

Best Options:

- The Retreat at Blue Lagoon: Located outside the city but worth mentioning for those seeking an indulgent experience, this luxury hotel offers access to the Blue Lagoon, private lagoons, and spa treatments.
   - The Reykjavik EDITION: A five-star hotel offering luxurious rooms, dining experiences, and a prime location near the Harpa Concert Hall.

Apartment Rentals and Airbnbs

Reykjavik has a wide range of apartment rentals and Airbnbs, which are ideal for families, long-term visitors, or travelers who prefer the comforts of home. Many of these accommodations are located in the downtown area or in quieter neighborhoods like Vesturbær and Hlíðar, offering both privacy and convenience.

Here's a detailed overview of luxury hotels in Reykjavik, Iceland, showcasing some of the finest accommodations that blend comfort, style, and exceptional service:

Luxury Hotels in Reykjavik

1. The Reykjavik EDITION

- Overview: Situated by the waterfront and near Harpa Concert Hall, this modern luxury hotel offers a unique blend of contemporary design and Icelandic aesthetics.
  - Highlights:
  - Rooms & Suites: Elegant rooms with floor-to-ceiling windows and bespoke furnishings.
  - Dining: On-site restaurants offering local and international cuisine.
  - Amenities: Rooftop bar, wellness center, and an exclusive spa.

2. Hotel Borg by Keahotels

- Overview: An iconic hotel in the heart of Reykjavik, Hotel Borg is known for its art deco elegance and historic charm.
  - Highlights:
  - Rooms & Suites: Beautifully designed rooms with luxurious amenities.
  - Dining: Borg Restaurant offers fine dining experiences.
  - Spa & Wellness: Offers a spa, sauna, and fitness center for relaxation.

3. Tower Suites Reykjavik

- Overview: Located on the top floors of a building, this exclusive hotel features luxurious suites with panoramic views of the city and surrounding landscapes.

- Highlights:
  - Suites: Nine lavish suites with modern decor and stunning views.
  - Service: Personalized concierge services tailored to guests' needs.
  - Experience: Ideal for couples looking for a romantic getaway.

4. The Retreat at Blue Lagoon

- Overview: Though not in Reykjavik, this luxury hotel is a must-visit for its exclusive access to the famous Blue Lagoon geothermal spa.
  - Highlights:
  - Rooms & Suites: Luxurious accommodations with views of the lagoon and surrounding lava fields.
  - Dining: Michelin-starred restaurant Moss offers Icelandic cuisine with a twist.
  - Spa: World-class spa with unique treatments inspired by the geothermal waters.

5. Sand Hotel by Keahotels

- Overview: This boutique hotel on Laugavegur, Reykjavik's main shopping street, combines modern luxury with a cozy atmosphere.
  - Highlights:
  - Rooms: Stylish rooms featuring warm Icelandic decor.
  - Dining: A bistro and bar with a selection of local and international dishes.
  - Location: Conveniently located near shops, cafes, and cultural attractions.

6. Reykjavik Konsulat Hotel by Hilton

- Overview: Set in a historic building, this hotel offers a luxurious experience with modern amenities and a central location.
  - Highlights:
  - Rooms & Suites: Spacious accommodations with chic decor and modern conveniences.
  - Dining: An in-house restaurant serving a mix of local and international cuisine.
  - Amenities: Wellness spa and fitness center for guests.

7. Black Pearl Apartment Hotel

- Overview: This upscale apartment hotel is ideal for travelers looking for luxury accommodations with the comforts of home.
  - Highlights:
  - Apartments: Fully equipped apartments with kitchens and stylish furnishings.
  - Service: Personalized concierge services to assist with reservations and local insights.
  - Location: Close to the Old Harbour and popular attractions.

8. Fosshotel Reykjavik

- Overview: The largest hotel in Iceland, Fosshotel Reykjavik offers modern comfort and a range of amenities.
  - Highlights:
  - Rooms: Stylish, comfortable rooms with modern decor.
  - Dining: A restaurant and bar serving a variety of dishes.

- Amenities: Conference facilities and a fitness center.

9. Alda Hotel Reykjavik

- Overview: Located on Laugavegur, Alda Hotel combines contemporary design with warm hospitality.
  - Highlights:
  - Rooms: Spacious rooms with sleek, modern designs.
  - Dining: A trendy restaurant offering a variety of dishes.
  - Wellness: A sauna and hot tub for relaxation after a day of exploring.

Here's a list of budget-friendly hostels in Reykjavik, Iceland, that offer affordable accommodations without compromising comfort and convenience:

Budget-Friendly Hostels in Reykjavik

1. Reykjavik Downtown HI Hostel

- Overview: Centrally located, this hostel is a great choice for travelers looking to explore Reykjavik on foot.
  - Highlights:
  - Dorms & Private Rooms: Offers a variety of room options, including shared dorms and private rooms.
  - Common Areas: Spacious common areas and a fully equipped kitchen.
  - Facilities: Free Wi-Fi, laundry facilities, and bike rentals available.

2. Kex Hostel

- Overview: Housed in an old biscuit factory, Kex Hostel combines a quirky atmosphere with modern amenities.
  - Highlights:
  - Dorms & Private Rooms: Features both dormitory-style and private accommodations.
  - Bar & Restaurant: On-site bar and restaurant serving local dishes and craft beers.
  - Social Atmosphere: Regular live music and events foster a vibrant community vibe.

3. HI Hostel Reykjavik

- Overview: Part of the Hostelling International network, this hostel provides a comfortable and social atmosphere.
  - Highlights:
  - Dorms & Private Rooms: Offers a range of options, from shared dorms to private family rooms.
  - Common Areas: Cozy lounges and a large kitchen for guest use.
  - Location: Close to the city center and various attractions.

4. Hlemmur Square

- Overview: A modern hostel located in a vibrant area, Hlemmur Square offers both hostel and hotel-style accommodations.
  - Highlights:
  - Rooms: Mix of dormitory and private rooms with contemporary decor.

- Café & Bar: On-site café and bar serving breakfast and snacks.
   - Public Transportation: Easy access to buses and the main shopping area.

5. The Capital Inn

- Overview: A budget-friendly hostel that offers both dormitory and private room options with a homey feel.
   - Highlights:
   - Accommodations: Comfortable dorms and private rooms with shared bathrooms.
   - Amenities: Fully equipped kitchen, common lounge, and a garden area.
   - Location: Close to downtown Reykjavik and the city's attractions.

6. Hostel B47

- Overview: Located in a quiet area near the city center, Hostel B47 provides a relaxed atmosphere for travelers.
   - Highlights:
   - Dorms & Private Rooms: Offers various accommodations, including family rooms.
   - Common Kitchen: Well-equipped kitchen for self-catering.
   - Facilities: Free Wi-Fi and communal lounge areas for socializing.

7. Galaxy Pod Hostel

- Overview: A unique, futuristic hostel offering pod-style accommodations that provide privacy in a social setting.
  - Highlights:
  - Pods: Individual sleeping pods in dormitory-style rooms with shared bathrooms.
  - Common Areas: Chill-out lounges and a kitchen area for guest use.
  - Location: Close to major attractions and public transport options.

8. Alda Hotel

- Overview: While primarily a hotel, Alda also offers budget-friendly rooms that appeal to hostel-goers seeking comfort without high costs.
  - Highlights:
  - Rooms: Comfortable and stylish rooms with modern amenities.
  - Facilities: Shared kitchen and common areas.
  - Social Atmosphere: A friendly atmosphere with opportunities to meet fellow travelers.

Unique Guesthouses in Reykjavik

1. Reykjavik Treasure B&B

- Overview: This cozy guesthouse, located in a historical building near the Old Harbour, offers a warm, intimate atmosphere.
  - Highlights:
  - Rooms: Individually decorated rooms with rustic charm and

modern comforts.
   - Breakfast: Complimentary homemade breakfast with local ingredients.
   - Location: Ideal for exploring central Reykjavik, with attractions like Harpa Concert Hall and Laugavegur street nearby.

2. House of the Spirits

- Overview: Set in a renovated historic building from 1913, this guesthouse blends traditional Icelandic architecture with modern touches.
   - Highlights:
   - Rooms & Apartments: Offers both rooms and self-catering apartments, perfect for longer stays.
   - Atmosphere: Each room has its own unique character with antique furniture and local art.
   - Location: Walking distance from the city center and the harbor.

3. Guesthouse Sunna

- Overview: A family-run guesthouse offering a welcoming environment right next to Hallgrímskirkja, Reykjavik's iconic church.
   - Highlights:
   - Rooms & Apartments: A variety of rooms from simple single rooms to spacious family apartments.
   - Facilities: Fully equipped kitchens available for guests, and a buffet breakfast is served each morning.
   - Location: Central, making it easy to explore the city's main landmarks.

4. Guesthouse Galtafell

- Overview: Housed in a historic building once home to a renowned Icelandic artist, Guesthouse Galtafell offers a combination of history, art, and comfort.
    - Highlights:
    - Rooms & Studios: Well-decorated rooms with a homely feel, including studio apartments with kitchenettes.
    - Historical Charm: The building itself is full of character, preserving the artistic legacy of its former owner.
    - Proximity: Located near Reykjavik's National Museum and the University of Iceland.

5. Loki 101 Guesthouse

- Overview: Named after the Norse god Loki, this guesthouse offers a quirky and budget-friendly stay near Hallgrímskirkja.
    - Highlights:
    - Rooms: Bright and simple rooms with shared bathroom facilities.
    - Common Areas: Guests have access to a shared kitchen and a cozy garden area.
    - Location: Prime location for exploring Reykjavik, with shops, cafes, and cultural sites just steps away.

6. Reykjavik Guesthouse

- Overview: A modern and minimalist guesthouse located close to Laugavegur, Reykjavik's main shopping street.
    - Highlights:

- Rooms: Comfortable, modern rooms with shared bathroom facilities.
  - Breakfast: Optional breakfast service available with a focus on local produce.
  - Affordability: A budget-friendly option for travelers seeking central accommodations.

7. Blue House B&B

- Overview: Located in the quiet seaside neighborhood of Seltjarnarnes, this charming guesthouse offers stunning views of the sea and mountains.
  - Highlights:
  - Rooms: Beautifully decorated rooms with cozy, Nordic touches.
  - Nature: Ideal for nature lovers, with views of Mount Esja and a chance to spot the Northern Lights in winter.
  - Distance: Just a 10-minute drive from downtown Reykjavik, providing a peaceful retreat close to the city.

8. Igdlo Guesthouse

- Overview: A family-owned guesthouse with a relaxed atmosphere, offering simple yet comfortable accommodations at a reasonable price.
  - Highlights:
  - Rooms: Clean, Scandinavian-style rooms with both private and shared bathrooms.
  - Common Areas: A fully equipped guest kitchen and a garden for relaxation.
  - Location: Conveniently located within walking distance of down-

town Reykjavik and major bus routes.

9. Guesthouse Pavi

- Overview: A no-frills guesthouse that offers comfortable and affordable rooms in a central location.
- Highlights:
- Rooms: Variety of rooms, from budget single rooms to larger family accommodations.
- Affordability: Great value for travelers on a budget who still want to stay close to the city's main attractions.
- Proximity: Situated near Laugavegur and Hlemmur Bus Station, making it easy to explore Reykjavik.

10. Reykjavik Lights Guesthouse

- Overview: A modern guesthouse inspired by the natural light patterns in Iceland, this property offers stylish and affordable accommodations.
- Highlights:
- Design: Contemporary design with a focus on clean lines and natural light.
- Rooms: Comfortable rooms with modern furnishings and private bathrooms.
- Amenities: Offers breakfast and is close to public transport for day trips outside Reykjavik.

Camping and Outdoor Lodging in Reykjavik

Reykjavik is not just a bustling city but also a gateway to some of the most scenic outdoor experiences in Iceland. For travelers who prefer staying closer to nature, the city and its surrounding areas offer excellent camping and outdoor lodging options. Here's a guide to the best camping spots and outdoor accommodations near Reykjavik:

1. Reykjavik Campsite

- Overview: This is the main campsite in Reykjavik, conveniently located just 3 km from the city center, making it an excellent base for exploring both Reykjavik and nearby attractions.
  - Highlights:
  - Facilities: Offers modern amenities like hot showers, a laundry room, Wi-Fi, and electricity hookups for campers.
  - Open Season: Open year-round, although services may be limited in winter.
  - Activities: Easily accessible to hiking trails, geothermal pools, and the city's main attractions.
  - Proximity: Close to Laugardalslaug geothermal pool and a large botanical garden.

2. Tjaldsvæðið Mosfellsbær Campsite

- Overview: Located just 15 minutes from Reykjavik, this campsite offers a more tranquil setting while still being close to the city.
  - Highlights:

- Scenery: Surrounded by mountains, including the iconic Mount Esja, this site provides a picturesque camping experience.
- Facilities: Equipped with restrooms, hot showers, and picnic tables. A great spot for nature lovers.
- Activities: Ideal for outdoor activities like hiking, with easy access to the start of Mount Esja's hiking trails.

3. Hafnarfjordur Campsite

- Overview: Located 10 km south of Reykjavik, Hafnarfjordur is a scenic campsite in a lava field, offering a unique outdoor lodging experience.
- Highlights:
- Facilities: Offers excellent amenities like a kitchen, showers, and barbecue areas. There are also cabins available for those who prefer more comfort.
- Geothermal Pools: Close to one of the local geothermal pools, where campers can relax in naturally heated waters after a day of outdoor exploration.
- Nature: Surrounded by lava fields, it's perfect for those looking for a serene and natural environment.

4. Heiðmörk Nature Reserve

- Overview: While not an official campsite, Heiðmörk Nature Reserve offers a stunning location for outdoor lodging enthusiasts who want to explore the natural landscape close to Reykjavik.
- Highlight:
- Activities: Known for its hiking and nature trails, visitors can enjoy walking through lush forests, along lakes, and past volcanic rock

formations.

- Outdoor Lodging: While camping is not officially permitted, outdoor lodging experiences such as glamping or private rentals are available nearby.

- Tranquility: Offers a peaceful escape from the city's bustle, with opportunities to see wildlife and enjoy birdwatching.

5. Glamping in the Golden Circle Area

- Overview: For those looking for a blend of luxury and nature, glamping sites just outside Reykjavik, particularly along the Golden Circle route, offer a unique outdoor experience.

- Highlights:

- Accommodations: Fully equipped glamping tents with comfortable beds, heating, and sometimes private bathrooms.

- Scenery: These sites are located near popular natural landmarks such as Thingvellir National Park, providing stunning views and outdoor adventure opportunities.

- Facilities: Many glamping sites offer organized tours, dining options, and relaxation areas.

6. Þingvellir National Park Camping

- Overview: While a bit further out from Reykjavik, camping at Thingvellir National Park is a must for outdoor enthusiasts. It's about a 40-minute drive from Reykjavik.

- Highlights:

- Scenery: Stay in one of Iceland's most historically and geologically significant sites. The park is a UNESCO World Heritage Site, famous

for its rift valley and stunning landscapes.
- Facilities: Basic amenities include restrooms and cold water; there are no showers on-site, making it more suited for rugged campers.
- Outdoor Activities: Hiking, diving/snorkeling in the Silfra fissure, and exploring the park's natural beauty are all popular activities here.

7. Akranes Campsite

- Overview: Akranes, a small town about 45 minutes from Reykjavik, offers a charming campsite close to the sea, ideal for those who enjoy a coastal environment.
- Highlights:
- Facilities: Full camping amenities, including showers, electricity, and cooking areas.
- Scenery: Located by the beach, offering beautiful views of the surrounding mountains and the Atlantic Ocean.
- Activities: Excellent location for bird watching, hiking, and exploring the town's lighthouses.

8. Outdoor Lodging in Hvalfjörður

- Overview: A beautiful fjord just an hour's drive from Reykjavik, Hvalfjörður is a great place for those looking for a more remote camping or outdoor lodging experience.
- Highlights:
- Remote Camping: While there are no official campsites, some landowners offer private camping or outdoor lodges in the area.
- Activities: Explore nearby waterfalls (including Glymur, Iceland's second-highest), go hiking, or enjoy kayaking in the fjord.

- Peaceful Setting: Ideal for those who want to get away from the tourist crowds and enjoy nature in solitude.

Practical Information

Language and Communication in Reykjavik

Reykjavik, like the rest of Iceland, is a bilingual and highly educated city where language and communication are rarely barriers for travelers. Here's a breakdown of what to expect and tips on communicating during your visit:

—-

1. Official Language: Icelandic

- Overview: Icelandic, a North Germanic language, is the official language of Iceland. It has its roots in Old Norse and has remained relatively unchanged for centuries. Although it might seem daunting, most signage, official documents, and websites also provide translations in English.
  - Fun Fact: The Icelandic alphabet contains some unique letters, such as "Þ" (thorn), pronounced like the "th" in "thing," and "Ð" (eth), pronounced like the "th" in "this."

2. English Proficiency

- English as a Second Language: Most Icelanders speak fluent English, particularly in Reykjavik. English is taught as a second language from an early age, and many people working in tourism, retail, and hospitality are well-versed in English.
  - Where English is Common: English is widely spoken in hotels, restaurants, tourist attractions, and public services. Maps, guides, and menus are usually available in both Icelandic and English.

—-

3. Other Languages

- Nordic Languages: Since Iceland is part of the Nordic countries, some Icelanders also understand other Nordic languages, like Danish and Norwegian, although Icelandic is distinct from these languages.
  - German, French, and Spanish: You may encounter some individuals who speak additional European languages, especially those working in the tourism industry. However, English remains the dominant second language in Reykjavik.

—-

4. Learning a Few Icelandic Phrases

While English is widely understood, making an effort to learn a few basic Icelandic phrases can enhance your experience and endear you to locals. Here are some useful expressions:
- Hello: "Halló" or "Góðan daginn" (good day)
- Goodbye: "Bless" or "Vertu blessaður"
- Thank you: "Takk"
- Yes: "Já"
- No: "Nei"
- Excuse me: "Afsakið"
- Do you speak English?: "Talarðu ensku?"

Locals often appreciate it when visitors make the effort to use these simple words, even if your pronunciation isn't perfect.

—-

5. Internet and Communication Apps

- Wi-Fi Availability: Free Wi-Fi is widely available across Reykjavik, including in cafes, restaurants, hotels, and public places. It's easy to stay connected and use translation apps or communication tools.

- Communication Apps: Apps like Google Translate can be helpful for instant translations of written Icelandic. For messaging, Icelanders use the same international platforms like WhatsApp, Facebook Messenger, and iMessage.

—-

6. Cultural Communication Tips

- Direct but Polite: Icelanders tend to communicate directly but respectfully. Conversations are usually straightforward, with less small talk compared to some other cultures.
 - Respect for Personal Space: Icelanders value personal space, so avoid standing too close during conversations.
 - Non-verbal Communication: Like many Northern European countries, body language in Iceland is reserved. A firm handshake is common when meeting someone for the first time.

—-

Currency and Payment Methods in Reykjavik

When traveling to Reykjavik, understanding the local currency and payment methods is essential for a smooth and stress-free experience. Here's a detailed guide on what to expect and how to manage your finances while exploring Iceland's capital.

—-

1. Icelandic Currency: The Icelandic Króna (ISK)

- Currency Symbol: ISK or kr
  - Currency Code: ISK
  - Coins: The Icelandic króna comes in 1, 5, 10, 50, and 100 kr coins.

- Banknotes: Banknotes are available in denominations of 500, 1,000, 2,000, 5,000, and 10,000 kr.

The Icelandic króna is the sole currency used in Iceland. You won't be able to use foreign currencies like the euro or US dollars, but exchanging your currency is straightforward.

—-

2. Exchanging Money

- Currency Exchange Locations: You can exchange foreign currency for Icelandic króna at Keflavik International Airport, banks, and certain hotels in Reykjavik. However, ATMs are widely available and typically offer better exchange rates than physical currency exchange services.
  - ATMs: You can easily withdraw ISK from ATMs around Reykjavik using international credit or debit cards. ATMs are common and available at banks, shopping centers, and convenience stores.
  - Currency Exchange Apps: It's helpful to use currency converter apps to check exchange rates and manage your budget in real-time.

—-

3. Cash or Card?

- Card Dominance: Iceland is a cashless society, and cards are accepted almost everywhere, including small shops, cafes, taxis, and even public restrooms. Many locals rarely carry cash and rely entirely on debit or credit cards for everyday transactions.

- Cashless Payments: Visa and MasterCard are the most widely accepted cards. American Express is less commonly used but still accepted in some locations. Contactless payments (tap-to-pay) are also widely supported.

- Carrying Cash: Although cards are the primary payment method, it's still a good idea to have a small amount of cash for emergencies or remote areas outside Reykjavik where card services might be unavailable.

—-

4. Tipping and Gratuities

- No Tipping Culture: Tipping is not expected in Iceland, as service charges are typically included in your bill. However, rounding up to the nearest amount or leaving a small tip for exceptional service is appreciated but not mandatory.

- Restaurants: In restaurants, your bill will already include service, so there's no need to add a tip unless you feel the service was outstanding.

- Taxis and Tours: It's uncommon to tip taxi drivers or tour guides, but again, rounding up the fare is always welcome.

—-

5. Mobile Payment Apps

- Apple Pay & Google Pay: Mobile payment apps like Apple Pay and Google Pay are widely accepted across Reykjavik, particularly in stores, restaurants, and transportation services that accept contactless payments.
  - Local Payment App – Aur: Iceland has a local mobile payment app called Aur, which some locals use for peer-to-peer payments. However, tourists typically won't need to use this, as international cards and mobile payment apps are more convenient.

—-

6. Tax-Free Shopping

- Tax Refund: Non-European travelers can claim a tax refund on purchases made in Iceland over a certain amount (typically ISK 6,000 or higher). The VAT (Value-Added Tax) in Iceland is 24%, and you can claim a portion of this back on certain goods like clothing, souvenirs, and other eligible items.
  - How It Works: When making a purchase, ask for a tax-free form at the store. Present this form, along with your receipts and goods, at the airport before departure to get your refund.
  - Refund Options: Refunds are available in cash (ISK, EUR, or USD) or can be credited back to your card.

—-

7. Budgeting and Cost of Living

- Cost Awareness: Reykjavik is known for being one of the more expensive cities in Europe, particularly when it comes to dining, accommodation, and activities. Having a budget plan in place before arrival can help manage expenses.
  - Currency Conversion: Be aware of the exchange rate to avoid overspending and be mindful of conversion fees your bank might charge for international transactions.

—-

Safety Tips and Health Precautions in Reykjavik, Iceland

Reykjavik is considered one of the safest cities in the world, with low crime rates and a well-maintained healthcare system. However, like in any travel destination, it's important to stay vigilant and take certain precautions to ensure a smooth and enjoyable experience. Below is a guide on safety tips and health precautions to keep in mind while visiting Reykjavik.

—-

PRACTICAL INFORMATION

1. General Safety in Reykjavik

- Low Crime Rate: Reykjavik has a low crime rate, and violent crime is rare. Most issues involve petty theft, so it's important to remain mindful of your belongings, especially in crowded tourist areas or when using public transportation.
  - Safe to Walk Around: Reykjavik is safe to explore day or night. The city center is compact and well-lit, so walking around at night generally isn't a concern, but always be cautious and aware of your surroundings.
  - Emergencies: In case of an emergency, the general emergency number in Iceland is 112. This number can be used to reach police, fire, ambulance, and search-and-rescue services.

—-

2. Outdoor Safety Tips

- Weather Preparedness: Iceland's weather can be unpredictable. Sudden rain, wind, or even snow can occur, so always check the forecast before heading out, especially for outdoor activities like hiking or exploring geothermal sites. Dress in layers and wear weather-appropriate gear such as waterproof clothing.
  - Hiking Safety: If you're hiking Mount Esja or venturing into the wilderness, let someone know your plans, check trail conditions, and be sure to bring enough water and food. Stick to marked trails and avoid hiking in bad weather.
  - Road Conditions: Iceland's roads, especially outside of Reykjavik, can be narrow, icy, or gravel-covered. When driving, stay within speed

limits, watch for animals crossing, and be cautious of changing weather conditions. Always rent a car equipped for winter if traveling during the colder months.

- Geothermal Safety: Iceland has numerous geothermal areas with hot springs and bubbling mud pools. Follow the marked paths and avoid touching or entering unmarked geothermal waters, as some are scalding hot and can cause burns.

—-

3. Health Precautions

- Healthcare System: Iceland has an excellent healthcare system. Emergency medical care is available in Reykjavik, and the main hospital, Landspítali University Hospital, provides services to locals and tourists alike.

- Travel Insurance: It is highly recommended to have travel insurance that covers medical emergencies, including outdoor activities like hiking or glacier tours.

- Pharmacies: Pharmacies (called "Apótek") are easy to find in Reykjavik, and most over-the-counter medications are available. For prescription drugs, you will need a valid prescription from a doctor.

- Emergency Health Services: In case of a medical emergency, dial 112 for immediate assistance. There are also walk-in health clinics in Reykjavik that tourists can visit for non-emergency medical issues.

- Water Quality: Tap water in Reykjavik is exceptionally clean and safe to drink. There is no need to buy bottled water, as Reykjavik's tap water is some of the purest in the world.

4. Safety During Outdoor Activities

- Glacier Hiking: If you plan to hike glaciers, always go with a certified guide. Glacier conditions can change quickly, and crevasses can be dangerous for inexperienced hikers. Ensure you have the proper gear and guidance.
    - Whale Watching and Boat Tours: When going on a whale-watching tour or other sea-related activities, ensure the tour operator follows safety regulations. Sea conditions can change rapidly, so it's important to wear the provided safety gear and listen to the crew's instructions.
    - Swimming in Hot Springs: While hot springs like the Blue Lagoon are well-maintained and safe for swimming, natural hot springs in more remote areas may vary in temperature. Test the water before entering, and follow any posted safety signs.

5. Northern Lights Viewing

- Cold Weather Preparedness: Viewing the Northern Lights requires standing outside, often in the cold night air. Dress warmly with insulated layers, and wear a hat, gloves, and waterproof boots. If you're part of a guided tour, the operator will usually provide safety instructions for staying comfortable and safe while outdoors for extended periods.
    - Driving in Winter: If you are driving to remote areas to view the Northern Lights, ensure your car is equipped with winter tires, and

consider hiring a guide if you're unfamiliar with Iceland's roads in winter conditions.

—-

6. Solo Travel Safety

- Solo Travel Friendly: Reykjavik is a great destination for solo travelers. The city's low crime rate and welcoming atmosphere make it a safe place to explore alone. Nevertheless, as a solo traveler, stay alert, share your itinerary with a trusted person, and keep emergency contacts handy.

—-

Environmental Awareness in Reykjavik, Iceland

Iceland is renowned for its unspoiled natural landscapes, and the country takes environmental conservation seriously. As a visitor to Reykjavik and the surrounding areas, it is important to be mindful of the environmental impact of your activities and to follow sustainable travel practices to preserve Iceland's beauty for future generations. Below is a guide to understanding and promoting environmental awareness during your visit to Reykjavik.

—-

PRACTICAL INFORMATION

1. Protecting Iceland's Fragile Ecosystem

- Respect Nature: Iceland's volcanic landscapes, glaciers, and geothermal areas are delicate ecosystems. Stay on marked paths and trails to avoid damaging vegetation, as some plants and mosses can take decades to recover from being disturbed.
   - Wildlife Conservation: Iceland is home to unique wildlife, including puffins, Arctic foxes, and whales. Avoid disturbing wildlife, keep a safe distance, and never feed or approach animals. Support sustainable whale-watching tours that respect marine life and adhere to conservation guidelines.
   - Geothermal Areas: Geothermal features like hot springs and geysers are sensitive to human impact. Always follow posted signs and avoid touching or entering geothermal pools that are not designated for bathing, as they can be dangerous and ecologically sensitive.

—-

2. Reducing Your Carbon Footprint

- Sustainable Transportation: Opt for eco-friendly transportation when possible. Reykjavik is walkable, and you can rent bikes to explore the city without contributing to carbon emissions. Use Reykjavik's efficient public transportation system instead of renting a car for short trips around the city.
   - Eco-Friendly Car Rentals: If you plan to rent a car, choose hybrid or electric vehicles when available. Many car rental agencies in Reykjavik offer environmentally conscious options, and Iceland's extensive

network of charging stations makes it easy to travel sustainably.

- Minimize Air Travel: Iceland is a popular stopover destination, but reducing short-haul flights by staying longer in Reykjavik or combining several activities in one trip can minimize your environmental impact.

—-

3. Responsible Waste Management

- Recycling and Waste Disposal: Iceland is dedicated to recycling, and you'll find recycling bins for plastic, paper, glass, and metals throughout Reykjavik. Dispose of waste in designated bins, and avoid littering, especially in natural areas.

- Plastic-Free Travel: Reduce your use of plastic by carrying reusable water bottles, shopping bags, and utensils. Tap water in Reykjavik is of exceptional quality, so you can refill your water bottle instead of buying bottled water.

- Leave No Trace: When hiking or exploring Iceland's wilderness, adhere to the "Leave No Trace" principles. Pack out all your trash, including food waste, and dispose of it properly when you return to the city.

—-

4. Energy Efficiency

- Renewable Energy: Iceland is a world leader in renewable energy, with nearly 100% of its electricity and heating coming from geothermal and hydropower sources. As a traveler, you can support Iceland's renewable energy goals by being mindful of energy usage in hotels or accommodations.
   - Eco-Friendly Accommodations: Many hotels and guesthouses in Reykjavik follow sustainable practices, such as using energy-efficient appliances, offering recycling options, and conserving water. Choose eco-certified accommodations when booking your stay.

—-

5. Supporting Sustainable Tourism

- Responsible Tours: Choose tour operators that prioritize sustainability and environmental responsibility. Many Icelandic companies offer eco-friendly tours, including small-group excursions, electric vehicle tours, and experiences that minimize impact on the environment.
   - Local and Sustainable Products: Support Icelandic artisans and businesses by purchasing locally-made products rather than imported goods. Look for shops and restaurants that source materials and ingredients from sustainable, local sources, helping to reduce the carbon footprint and support the community.

—-

6. Water Conservation

- Conserving Hot Water: While Iceland is blessed with abundant geothermal energy, it's still important to use hot water responsibly. Limit the length of your showers, and turn off taps when brushing your teeth or shaving.

 - Water Quality: Reykjavik's tap water is not only safe to drink but also one of the purest in the world. Avoid buying bottled water and instead use a refillable bottle during your stay.

—-

7. Avoiding Over-Tourism

- Visiting Popular Sites Responsibly: Reykjavik and nearby attractions like the Blue Lagoon, Golden Circle, and Thingvellir National Park are popular tourist destinations. To help avoid the negative impacts of over-tourism, consider visiting during the off-peak season or visiting lesser-known attractions that are equally beautiful but less crowded.

 - Respecting Cultural Heritage: Iceland's history and culture are deeply connected to its landscapes. Treat cultural sites with respect, including historical landmarks, museums, and traditional Icelandic farms. Don't remove stones, plants, or other natural materials as souvenirs, and avoid graffiti or vandalism at cultural heritage sites.

Conclusion

Summary of Must-Visit Places in Reykjavik, Iceland

Reykjavik is a city rich in history, culture, and natural beauty. Below is a summary of the top must-visit places and experiences to explore during your trip:

1. Hallgrímskirkja

- Iconic Landmark: The towering church offers stunning architecture and panoramic views of Reykjavik from the top of its steeple.

2. Harpa Concert Hall

- Cultural Hub: A striking glass building that hosts concerts, events, and exhibitions, while offering breathtaking views of the harbor.

3. Sun Voyager

- Sculpture by the Sea: A beautiful steel sculpture resembling a Viking ship, symbolizing dreams of undiscovered territory and adventure.

4. National Museum of Iceland

- Cultural History: Discover Iceland's rich history from the Settlement Era to modern times with unique exhibits and artifacts.

5. Reykjavik City Hall

- Modern Architecture: Situated on the shores of Tjörnin lake, it's an excellent place to learn about the city's history, art, and politics.

6. Mount Esja

- Hiking and Nature: A popular hiking spot just outside Reykjavik, offering various trails and spectacular views of the surrounding area.

7. Viðey Island

- Nature and Art: Explore this peaceful island via ferry to see sculptures, historical sites, and picturesque nature trails.

8. Blue Lagoon

- Geothermal Spa: A world-renowned geothermal pool with milky blue waters set amidst a lava field – a quintessential Icelandic experience.

9. Laugardalslaug

- Local Hot Spring: Reykjavik's largest public swimming pool, featuring geothermal baths, waterslides, and steam rooms.

10. Thingvellir National Park

- World Heritage Site: A natural wonder where you can see the rift between the North American and Eurasian tectonic plates, rich in historical significance.

11. Golden Circle

- Scenic Route: A must-see day trip featuring Þingvellir National Park, Gullfoss Waterfall, and the Geysir geothermal area.

12. Snaefellsnes Peninsula

- Diverse Landscapes: Known as "Iceland in Miniature," this peninsula showcases volcanoes, glaciers, lava fields, and stunning coastal cliffs.

13. Seljalandsfoss and Skógafoss Waterfalls

- Spectacular Waterfalls: Two of Iceland's most famous waterfalls, where you can walk behind Seljalandsfoss and marvel at Skógafoss' mighty cascade.

14. Reynisfjara Black Sand Beach

- Unique Coastal Beauty: Famous for its black volcanic sands and basalt columns, with dramatic ocean waves and sea stacks.

15. Silfra Fissure

- Snorkeling and Diving: An underwater paradise in Þingvellir National Park, known for its crystal-clear water between two tectonic plates.

16. Northern Lights Viewing

- Aurora Borealis: Chase the magical Northern Lights in Reykjavik or venture out to more remote areas for a dazzling display.

—-

These highlights showcase Reykjavik's unique blend of natural beauty, cultural landmarks, and outdoor adventures, making it a vibrant destination for all kinds of travelers.

CONCLUSION

Final Tips for Travelers to Reykjavik, Iceland

As you prepare for your journey to Reykjavik, here are some essential tips to enhance your experience:

1. Plan for the Weather

- Layer Up: Iceland's weather can be unpredictable, even in summer. Dress in layers to stay warm and comfortable.
  - Waterproof Gear: Bring a sturdy waterproof jacket and shoes, especially if you're exploring waterfalls or hiking.

2. Be Ready for Daylight Changes

- Midnight Sun (Summer): In summer, daylight lasts nearly 24 hours, so consider bringing an eye mask to sleep comfortably.
  - Limited Daylight (Winter): During winter, daylight is short, so plan your outdoor activities accordingly.

3. Respect Nature

- Stay on Marked Paths: Iceland's fragile landscape needs protection. Stick to designated paths to avoid damaging the ecosystem.
  - Follow Safety Signs: Whether near geothermal areas or glaciers, always heed safety warnings.

4. Budget for High Costs

- Cost of Living: Reykjavik can be expensive, especially for dining and accommodation. Plan and budget for higher-than-average prices.
    - Tax Refund: If you're purchasing items, be aware of VAT refunds available to tourists on certain purchases.

5. Learn Basic Icelandic Phrases

- While most Icelanders speak excellent English, knowing a few Icelandic phrases can be a fun way to connect with locals.
    - "Takk" (Thank you)
    - "Halló" (Hello)
    - "Já" (Yes)
    - "Nei" (No)

6. Pack a Swimsuit

- Geothermal Pools: Iceland is famous for its geothermal spas, so don't forget a swimsuit. Whether you visit the Blue Lagoon or local hot springs, it's an integral part of the experience.

7. Use Contactless Payment

- Card Payments: Iceland is highly card-friendly, and you can use contactless payment nearly everywhere, making it convenient for travelers to avoid carrying too much cash.

CONCLUSION

8. Download Useful Apps

- Maps and Transportation: Consider downloading offline maps (such as Google Maps) or apps like Straeto for public transportation schedules.
    - Aurora Forecast: If you're chasing the Northern Lights, an app like "My Aurora Forecast" can help track their visibility.

9. Book in Advance

- Tours and Attractions: Many popular tours, such as whale watching or Northern Lights hunts, can fill up fast. Book these experiences ahead of time to secure a spot.

10. Enjoy the Local Culture

- Slow Pace: Icelanders are known for their relaxed, slow pace of life. Embrace this laid-back atmosphere and enjoy the moments of tranquility, whether exploring Reykjavik or soaking in a hot spring.

—-

By following these tips, you'll be well-prepared to make the most of your adventure in Reykjavik and beyond! Safe travels!

Made in the USA
Columbia, SC
09 January 2025